KOSOVO
WHAT EVERYONE NEEDS TO KNOW

Also by the Author

Kosovo: War and Revenge

*The Serbs: History, Myth,
and the Destruction of Yugoslavia*

KOSOVO

What Everyone Needs to Know

TIM JUDAH

OXFORD
UNIVERSITY PRESS

2008

OXFORD
UNIVERSITY PRESS

Oxford University Press, Inc., publishes works that further
Oxford University's objective of excellence
in research, scholarship, and education.

Oxford   New York
Auckland   Cape Town   Dar es Salaam   Hong Kong   Karachi
Kuala Lumpur   Madrid   Melbourne   Mexico City   Nairobi
New Delhi   Shanghai   Taipei   Toronto

With offices in
Argentina   Austria   Brazil   Chile   Czech Republic   France   Greece
Guatemala   Hungary   Italy   Japan   Poland   Portugal   Singapore
South Korea   Switzerland   Thailand   Turkey   Ukraine   Vietnam

Copyright © 2008 by Tim Judah

Published by Oxford University Press, Inc.
198 Madison Avenue, New York, New York 10016

www.oup.com

Oxford is a registered trademark of Oxford University Press

Library of Congress Cataloging-in-Publication Data
Judah, Tim, 1962–
Kosovo : what everyone needs to know / Tim Judah.
p.   cm.
Includes bibliographical references and index.
ISBN 978-0-19-537673-9; 978-0-19-537345-5 (pbk.)
1. Kosovo (Republic)—History.   2. Serbs—Kosovo (Republic)—History.
3. Albanians—Kosovo (Republic)—History.   I. Title.
DR2082.J83 2008
949.71—dc22   2008021141

1 3 5 7 9 8 6 4 2

Printed in the United States of America
on acid-free paper

CONTENTS

Acknowledgments   vii
Author's Note   ix
Preface: Why Kosovo?   xiii
Abbreviations   xxi

 1   Albanians   1
 2   Serbs   12
 3   Creating History   18
 4   From Dardania to Yugoslavia   30
 5   Kosovo in Yugoslavia   42
 6   From the Golden Age to the Memorandum   55
 7   The Milošević-Rugova Years   64
 8   The War   75
 9   Kosovo after 1999   93
10   March 2004 and the Ahtisaari Plan   108
11   Kosovo and the Region   117
12   Kosovo and the World   127
13   Not the Last Chapter: Independence   140

Notes   153
Bibliography   167
Index   171

ACKNOWLEDGMENTS

Thanks to Rosie and my family. To John Peet, the Europe Editor of the *Economist*. To my agent, Natasha Fairweather, and to Tim Bent at Oxford University Press. To Joshua Haymann for the cover. To all my friends at, and around, Balkan Insight (www.balkaninsight.com/). Likewise to my friends at and around the European Stability Initiative (www.esiweb.org/). To Zoran Culafić, Veton Surroi, Braca Grubačić of VIP, Migjen Kelmendi, Sonja Ristić, and many, many more, including, and especially, one who popped up on Skype at just the right time.

This book is dedicated to my Aunt Claire.

AUTHOR'S NOTE

As a journalist I have covered the former Yugoslavia since 1991, so I have been traveling to and from Kosovo ever since then. Over that time it has changed beyond recognition, but many of the problems it faces today remain essentially the same.

This book has no pretensions. It aims to do exactly what it says on the cover—to tell you all you need to know about Kosovo. If you end up wondering why this or that is not here, that is because this book is not aimed at specialists, but rather the idea is just to give general readers, especially if they are new to this area, a straightforward introduction.

What is contained here is based on all I have learned in my years of covering Kosovo and the Western Balkans. Unless otherwise stated, quotes are from my interviews. At the end of the book is a short bibliography, which includes my previous book on Kosovo and my book on the Serbs. Two other books deserve special mention here, for in their different ways they are outstanding. The first is Noel Malcolm's *Kosovo: A Short History*. The second is *Le Piège du Kosovo* by Jean-Arnault Dérens, an updated version of his earlier *Kosovo, anneé zéro*. Dérens is the Francophone world's top Balkan expert. He runs the website, *Le Courrier des Balkans* (http://balkans .courriers.info/).

A problem is the issue of names. Let's deal with Kosovo first. It is "Kosovo" here, not the Albanian "Kosova," because that is what it is called in English, just as "Italy" is not Italia. Maybe, over the years that will change but for the moment it is that. When it comes to names within Kosovo, though, everything becomes more complicated. Most towns and villages have a Serbian and an Albanian name. So it is "Priština" in Serbian and "Prishtina" (or "Prishtinë," depending on the context) in Albanian. But some places have totally different names: for example, "Uroševac" is the Serbian name for the place Albanians call "Ferizaj." A few places have exactly the same name in both languages, for example, Prizren.

When I wrote my first book about Kosovo, just after the war of 1999—when Serbia lost control of most of Kosovo—it still seemed okay to use the Serbian names, which were more familiar to an English-speaking readership. Now that is no longer the case, and many books and documents use both. This is ungainly, but unless you are careful, conspiracy theorists will *always* sniff out bias where there is none. So, I have attempted to strike a balance, sometimes using both, especially when first mentioned, sometimes choosing between one or the other, depending in part on the context. For example, I describe the Serbian Orthodox Patriarchate as being in Peć, rather than "Peja." The most commonly used place name in the book is Priština/Prishtina. It would be too odd to keep alternating it, so for here only I decided on *Economist* English usage: plain Pristina, no "š" and no "h." Mitrovica works in both languages, although officially it is "Kosovska Mitrovica" in Serbian. The mines are sometimes in Trepča (Serbian) and sometimes in Trepça (Albanian). It would be more than pedantic to keep writing "Trepča/Trepça." To reduce the number of name repetitions, I have minimized the number of double names used for places outside Kosovo. Anyone who tries to work out a failsafe system on names, except if they use just one language or the other, is wasting their time.

PREFACE: WHY KOSOVO?

Why Kosovo? If location is all when it comes to property then geography counts when it comes to people and countries. Kosovo is a tiny place with a tiny population, yet it was the reason that NATO fought its first war. Recently it has been a major subject of international discord, especially between European and American leaders on the one side and a resurgent Russia on the other. If Kosovo were in central Asia, or Africa, or in the Caucasus, this would not have been the case. Kosovo counts because it is in the middle of Europe. On February 17, 2008, it declared independence, becoming the world's newest and most controversial of states.

Look at the map. Kosovo and the rest of the Western Balkans are countries that are now surrounded by the territory of two of the most important and powerful organizations on the planet. On every side the region is enveloped by the European Union and NATO. So Kosovo and its neighborhood are not some place out there in Europe's backyard, but rather they constitute its inner courtyard. Nobody wants trouble here. They want peace and quiet, and good and reliable neighbors, not noisy, destitute troublemakers.

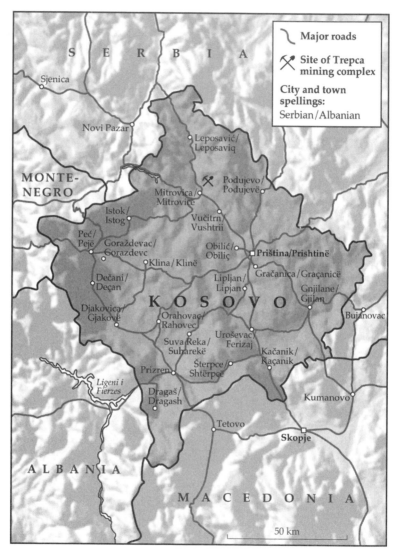

Kosovo (*Map by Phil Kenny*)

That is one huge reason that they matter. If they are allowed to become a black hole, or perhaps one should say revert to being a black hole, as during the wars of the 1990s, then what will this mean? A free trade zone for organized crime, traffickers, terrorists, and so on, not to mention the possibility of a return to conflict. Europe already has a problem coping with waves of desperate illegal migrants fleeing poverty from around the globe. But, in Kosovo and the Western Balkans, Europeans have, with the toolkit of EU integration, powerful means at their disposal to do something about this. Whether or not they succeed remains to be seen.

This region only became a proper enclave, or what is often called the "Balkan Ghetto," in January 2007, when Bulgaria and Romania joined the EU. They joined NATO in 2004 along with other former communist countries, and are also now preparing to join Schengen Europe, the vast passport-free zone that now stretches from Lisbon to Tallinn and Palermo to Reykjavik. So, except for Croats, all citizens of the Western Balkans need visas to go more or less anywhere in Europe. And of course there is the euro; the currency of 15 states plus Montenegro and Kosovo and, de facto, of Bosnia too, whose own currency is pegged to it. Whichever way you look at it, Kosovo and the Western Balkans are being surrounded and fenced in by all the institutions of modern Europe and what is called Euro-Atlantic integration. Contrast that with Afghanistan or Iraq, or indeed any other region either in conflict or emerging from it.

A word of clarification: What do we mean by the "Western Balkans"? This expression is used to describe the states of the former Yugoslavia, minus Slovenia, which is now an EU and NATO member, plus Albania. Slovenia apart, the former Yugoslav states are Kosovo, Serbia, Macedonia, Bosnia and

The Western Balkans Today (*Map by Peter Winfield*)

Hercegovina, Montenegro, and Croatia. Their combined population is rather small, about 22 million. Of that number, roughly 2 million live in Kosovo. Since no proper census has been conducted there for decades, no one knows for sure.

When Yugoslavia was destroyed in the early 1990s and war engulfed the region, hundreds of thousands of refugees were sent fleeing northward. In 1999, during the Kosovo war, some 850,000 people fled or were ethnically cleansed—forced to abandon their homes—from the territory. However, ever since the end of the Balkan wars, the region has made huge strides in restoring normality. Indeed, for all their problems, the postwar Balkans are a success story, especially when contrasted with other postconflict areas of the world. This progress is rarely reflected in the global media because it is not a very sexy tale to tell and besides, ever since 9/11, the world has changed and there have been other things to report on.

Despite this progress, though, one huge issue has remained a major apple of discord since the end of the armed conflicts: Kosovo. With its declaration of independence many people, especially its Albanians, hoped that this would be the end of the story. But just as we know that there is no end of history, there is also, of course, no end to Kosovo's either. Simply put, a chapter closed and a new one opened. It is the way that this chapter opened, the way that it came to independence, that is the second big reason, apart from geography, that Kosovo is important. When the Soviet Union disintegrated in 1991 its 15 constituent republics simply became new states. When Czechoslovakia was dissolved, the two new countries that succeeded it in 1993 were its two already existing federal units. Until Kosovo's declaration of independence, and subsequent recognition by the United States and most EU countries, the same story was repeated, albeit with much violence, in Yugoslavia.

When this country had been reconstituted in the wake of the Second World War it was reborn, not as the unitary state it had been before that war, but as a federation of six republics. Kosovo was not one of them. It was made a province of Serbia. From this several questions arise. Does the fact that the first sub-republican unit of a former communist state to be recognized as independent have implications elsewhere—for example, for the so-called frozen conflicts of the former Soviet Union? And what about elsewhere? As Kosovo has become an independent state without the consent of Serbia, does this have ramifications for separatists and their foes elsewhere, from Quebec to Tibet to Kurdistan via Spain's Basque country and Aceh in Indonesia?

The aim of this book is just to tell Kosovo's story, to lay out the facts, where these can be established, or otherwise the conflicting arguments, in order to give the reader an introduction to the country, its people, its problems and those of the rest of the region. With regard to the latter it is very important to set the story of Kosovo, past and present, within the context of the Balkans and now as part of a wider Europe. Kosovo is not an island. What happens there affects its neighbors and vice versa. Likewise, it is important to outline some of the major arguments that have accompanied Kosovo's independence. The most salient of these is the question of the right to self-determination, invoked by the Kosovo Albanians, as opposed to the right of the territorial integrity of states, invoked by Serbia.

For many Serbs, Kosovo's declaration of independence and subsequent recognition have been traumatic. Kosovo has always held a special place in the hearts and history of the Serbian people. Albanians, they believe, have stolen something that they regard as rightfully theirs. For the vast majority of the people who live in Kosovo today though, that is to say the Albanians, independence is the righting of a historical wrong, which is to say the Serbian conquest (Serbs say "liberation") of Kosovo in 1912. Serbs have argued that Kosovo is the heart of Serbia. If that is the case, retort Albanians, then the Serbian heart beats in a foreign body.

ABBREVIATIONS

CFSP	Common Foreign and Security Policy
ESDP	European Security and Defence Policy
ESI	European Stability Initiative
EU	European Union
EULEX	EU Rule of Law Mission in Kosovo
EUSR	EU Special Representative
ICO	International Civilian Office
ICR	International Civilian Representative
IMF	International Monetary Fund
LDK	Democratic League of Kosova
LPK	Popular Movement for Kosova
KFOR	Kosovo Force
KK	Kosovo Committee
KLA	Kosovo Liberation Army
KPC	Kosovo Protection Corps
KPS	Kosovo Police Service
KVM	Kosovo Verification Mission
NATO	North Atlantic Treaty Organisation
OSCE	Organization for Security and Cooperation in Europe

SAA   Stabilization and Association Agreement
SRSG   Special Representative of the Secretary General
UN   United Nations
UNHCR   UN High Commissioner for Refugees
UNMIK   UN Interim Administration Mission in Kosovo

KOSOVO

WHAT EVERYONE NEEDS TO KNOW

1

ALBANIANS

Although the focus of this book is Kosovo, it is also about the people of the Western Balkans, especially the Albanians and the Serbs, who do not fit neatly into the boundaries of the states that have come to exist today. More than that, it would make no sense to examine the history and politics of modern Kosovo without an understanding of this. Kosovo's Albanians are only a part of the wider Albanian nation—although today there is some debate as to whether, or to what extent, recent history has molded a distinct Kosovo Albanian identity, over and above a simply regional one. It is also important to understand the regional demographics because many argue that the current Balkan borders are illogical and should be redrawn to take ethnic realities into consideration. This may or may not be desirable, but to follow or take part in the debate it is crucial to know where people, and in this case Albanians, actually live.

The first questions we need to address are also the hardest. How many Albanians are there and where are they? The Balkan upheavals of the last two decades mean that for Kosovo and Albania there are very few reliable figures. For example, in 1981, the last census in which Kosovo Albanians participated, the total population of the province was given as 1.58 million, of whom 1.22 million or 77.4 percent were Albanians and 236,526 or 14.9 percent were Serbs and Montenegrins. A decade later the Albanians of Kosovo boycotted the census. Officials therefore estimated their number to be 1.6 million or 82.2 percent of a total population of 1.97 million, of whom 215,346 or 10.9 percent were Serbs and Montenegrins.[1] Albanians believe that in that count their numbers were deliberately underestimated. While the 1981 census was conducted under the auspices of the then Kosovo Albanian–dominated authorities, the 1991 one was not. So one factor that could be manipulated by either side in the hunt for the "right" statistics is how Roma—Gypsies, for example— were prevailed upon to identify themselves if not as Roma, since in Kosovo some speak Albanian, some Serbian.

In 2003 the Statistical Office of Kosovo, working under the auspices of the United Nations, estimated that there were some 1.9 million people in Kosovo, of whom 88 percent were Albanians and 7 percent were Serbs.[2] In their report of 2008, which was based on surveys and estimates done up to 2006 but not a proper census, they said that there were 2.1 million people resident in Kosovo and 586,543 outside, although they also said that without a census, "it is really hard to provide strong and reliable data."[3] Their website, but not the report, showed the following: Albanians constituted 92 percent of the population, Serbs 5.3 percent, and others 2.7 percent.[4]

What all this highlights is just how confusing the picture is, and why both Serbian and Albanian leaders may not want a new census, fearing what it might show, that is, that there could be far fewer of both people in Kosovo today than they make out.

Working out how many people are outside Kosovo is even more difficult than finding out how many there are inside it today. In the mid-1990s some half a million Kosovars were estimated to be living abroad. That figure cannot be less today, even though at least 100,000 Kosovo Albanians who had lived in Germany have returned since NATO's intervention in 1999.[5] Also, the Kosovo Statistical Office figure does not specify whether it includes Serbs abroad in their number of citizens abroad, especially those in Serbia who fled or were ethnically cleansed after 1999. The bulk of the Kosovo Albanian diaspora is in Switzerland, Germany, Austria, and Scandinavia but many Kosovars have also headed to Britain, the United States, and elsewhere. One reason why it is hard to estimate their numbers is because, as refugees or asylum seekers, they were listed as coming from Serbia and Montenegro, hence it was hard to distinguish them from Serbs and others and also from economic migrants from Albania claiming to be political refugees from Kosovo.

While many Kosovo Albanians now have citizenship of the countries where they live, most also retain Kosovo papers. Therefore, until some serious research is conducted, the official number of Albanians in Kosovo will fluctuate, depending on the source—from well under to well over 2 million. For that reason the rule of thumb used by foreign journalists and in many international documents, appears to be to use an estimate of 2 million, with the Albanians constituting some 90 percent of that number, Serbs 6 percent, and other minorities—Roma, Bosniaks, Goranis, and others—the rest.

While the vast majority of Albanians in the former Yugoslavia are in Kosovo, there are several other regions in which they also live. The second most important area of Albanian settlement is in western Macedonia, in an arc of land that begins at Struga, on Lake Ohrid, and stretches north, first along the Albanian and then the Kosovo border, taking in the towns of Debar, Tetovo, and Gostivar, then curving round to Skopje, the Macedonian capital, and villages close to its airport. While these areas have long been Albanian populated (though they are not all contiguous), Macedonians and Albanians used to live in closer proximity to one another and in more mixed communities than they do today.[6] For more than two decades a process of ethnic separation has continued apace, so that, for example, Albanians now live mostly in the northern part of Skopje and Macedonians in the south.

While ethnic tensions have decreased since the brief conflict of 2001, which pitted Kosovo-supported Albanian guerrillas against the Macedonian police and army, and Albanians and Macedonians work and do business together, there is little love lost between the communities. Macedonians fear that eventually Albanians will seek to break away from Macedonia and join a Greater Albania or a Greater Kosovo, while Albanians do not indentify with the state, not feeling it to be really their own. In 2002 a census found that there were 509,083 Albanians in Macedonia, making them some 25 percent of a population of just over 2 million.[7] Still, exact figures are hard to determine. Albanians in Macedonia have always had close relations, family and otherwise, with Kosovo. Many have papers issued by both Kosovo and Macedonia, while a certain, undetermined number from Kosovo who live in Macedonia do not have Macedonian citizenship. Like Kosovo Albanians, large numbers of Macedonian Albanians live and work abroad. The border between Kosovo and Macedonia is also no barrier for certain segments of the population. Academics, for example, frequently switch jobs between universities in Kosovo and Albanian-speaking posts in universities in Macedonia. Likewise, important Albanian politicians have alternated between jobs and roles in Kosovo and Macedonia.

To the north of Macedonia, but in the area contiguous with the arc of Albanian settlement and hard on the border of Kosovo and Serbia, lies another region inhabited by Albanians. This part of south Serbia is loosely referred to as the Preševo Valley, though actually Albanians live in three municipalities here: Preševo/Presheva, Bujanovac/Bujanoc, and Medvedja/Medvegja, the latter of which is not really in the valley. According to the 2002 census, some 61,647 Albanians live in Serbia (not including Kosovo), of whom some 57,600 live in these municipalities. Albanians constitute 89 percent of Preševo's population, 54.6 percent of Bujanovac's people, and 36 percent of those of Medvedja.[8]

Albanians often refer to this area as Eastern Kosovo and make reference to the fact that until the borders were drawn after the Second World War, traditionally much of it was considered part of Kosovo. In 1959 the small region of Lešak/ Leshak, which until then had been in Serbia proper, was added to northern Kosovo. The main reason for the Preševo border being drawn where it was, was to ensure that the main road and rail links from Belgrade to Skopje and Thessalonika, which pass through the Preševo Valley, should always be under Serbian control. By contrast, the point of adding a Serbian-inhabited region to the north of Kosovo was to make sure there were more Serbs in the province. Apart from the Preševo Valley there are also a few thousand ethnic Albanians who have long lived elsewhere in Serbia, where they tend to keep a low profile.

According to the 2003 census, the number of Albanians in Montenegro, which declared independence in June 2006, is 31,163, which represents 5.03 percent of a total population of 620,145.[9] Albanians in Montenegro have long been far better integrated into its society than Albanians in other parts of the former Yugoslavia. A small number live near the border of Kosovo, but the vast majority of them live either in overwhelmingly Albanian-inhabited Ulcinj/Ulqin, close to the Albanian border, or in Tuzi/Tuz. The former is traditionally a town of seafarers and, in more recent times, the holiday resort of choice of the former Yugoslav Albanians. Tuzi is close to the Montenegrin capital Podgorica. This region historically had close links with the town of Shkodër/Skadar just over the border in Albania. Historically Shkodër was a bastion of Albanian Catholicism, and so many Tuzi Albanians are Catholics too.

Three other points about Tuzi Albanians. There was a tradition in Tuzi that Albanians and Orthodox Montenegrins could be part of the same clan or tribe, something that language and religion would have ruled out elsewhere. Albanians from here also have a tradition of emigrating to the United States, as opposed to parts of Europe, and so have close links there. In recent years its Albanians have demanded that Tuzi, which has its own town council but is still part of Podgorica municipality, form a separate and hence Albanian-dominated one. Montenegrins fiercely oppose this move, fearing that it would be but an opening act in a long-term game plan to divide the region off from the country and join a future Greater Albania.

If the numbers of Montenegrin and Macedonian Albanians are a little clearer than those of Kosovo, perhaps most surprising is that the least clear figure of all is how people live in Albania itself, given that it is a state. In 2004 the Albanian Institute of Statistics estimated the country's population to be 3.1 million, which was exactly the same as in 1990.[10] Yet some 600,000 people are believed to have left since 1991 and to be working or living in Greece, some 250,000 in Italy, and another 200,000 or so elsewhere. Meanwhile, Albanians in Albania have continued to have plenty of children and a proportion of those living abroad have returned, but this still means that the real figure is uncertain. However, a credible estimate at the time of the elections in 2007 put the resident population at 2.7 million. Even more unclear are the figures for Albanians in countries that have long played host to its diaspora, such as the United States and Turkey, where up to 3 million people of Albanian descent may live.

The oldest of the Albanian diasporas are the Arbëresh, whose numbers today are diminished but who historically have played an important role. This Christian community in southern Italy is descended from Albanians who fled the invading Ottoman Turks in the 15th and 16th centuries. Small communities still exist in certain regions, speaking and preserving their own archaic Albanian.

Northern Greece used to be home to large numbers of Muslim Albanians, especially that area around Ioannina, which was once a predominantly Albanian town. Albanians call it "Janina" and the region "Çamëria." Its Albanians left or fled in three waves. First during the Balkan wars of 1912 and 1913, which left them outside the borders of the new Albania; second at the time of the population exchanges formalized in the Lausanne Treaty of 1923, which were mostly between Greece and Turkey; and finally toward the end of the Second World War as the Greeks accused them of collaboration first with Mussolini's Fascist Italy and then with the Nazis.[11]

Having described where Albanians are, it is important to outline some of their key characteristics. We have noted that some Albanians in Montenegro and Shkodër are Catholic. In Kosovo, in 2000, there were estimated to be around 60,000 Albanian Catholics, although this figure could be higher. There were also a very few Orthodox Albanians in Kosovo.

Generally speaking Albanians are a very secular people. Having said that, the overwhelming majority of Kosovo Albanians are of Muslim background. Likewise the vast majority of Macedonian Albanians are also Muslims, though their most famous daughter, Mother Teresa, born Agnes Gonxha Bojaxhiu in Skopje in 1910, was one of the late 20th century's most famous Catholics. In 1967 Enver Hoxha, Albania's communist dictator, declared Albania to be the world's first atheist state and religion was henceforth "abolished."

That heritage means that even now, long after the demise of communism in Albania, it is impossible to give precise figures of the religious background of the country's people, as many of them come from families that have long intermarried, a phenomenon that is far less common in Kosovo. When pressed however, Albanians in Albania estimate that somewhere between two-thirds and 80 percent of the country's citizens have a Muslim background or regard themselves as Muslim, while the rest are either Catholics, especially in the north, or Orthodox, especially in the south.

The Sunni Muslim background of most Albanians is complicated by the fact that, historically, Albania and the Albanians were a stronghold of the liberal, Sufi, Bektashi sect, regarded as heretical by orthodox Muslims. The strength of Bektashism, though it varied regionally, helps explain why Albanians tend to have a more relaxed view of religion than most other Muslim peoples. In the wake of the collapse of communism in Albania and since the war in Kosovo, Arab and Islamic charities and foundations have attempted to proselytize a more intolerant form of Islam among Albanians but, for the most part, they have met with little success.

So, does religion matter? Whenever Albanians address this issue it becomes a matter of pride, but also a cliché, to quote a line from a poem of Pashko Vasa, a 19th-century Catholic writer, who said that "the religion of the Albanians is Albanianism."[12] He meant that the identity of Albanians did not derive from their religion, as it did for other peoples in the Balkans. Thus the core of Serbian identity is, whether one is religious or not, entwined with the Serbian Orthodox Church, just as the Greek soul, identity, and history are entwined with their church. In Bosnia, to be a Bosniak means having a Muslim background, and for Croats the Catholic church is the key to understanding what makes them Croats, as opposed to Bosniaks or Serbs.

This point is key, as is the element of language. Albanian is the one thing that all Albanians have in common, despite regional variations between the Gheg dialect of the north, which includes Kosovo, and the Tosk dialect of the south. In this sense what makes an Albanian an Albanian stands in direct contradiction to what makes a Serb a Serb, a Bosniak a Bosniak, and a Croat a Croat, since whatever they chose to call their languages now, in essence they all speak the same, bar regional variations. So, while language and a shared identity define who is an Albanian, be they from Kosovo or from Albania or from anywhere else, it is religion that has defined the other nations of the Balkans.

It had to be this way. Albanians came late to the development of an all-embracing national identity. One major reason for this was because, during the long centuries of Ottoman domination, when the majority converted to Islam, there was no national church, as in the Serb or Greek cases, to nurture a separate nationhood. Second, as Muslims, many Albanians, especially if they were not in Albania or Kosovo, prospered under the Ottoman Empire. More than 40 Albanians served as grand viziers to the sultan, and Albanian communities flourished in Istanbul, in Egypt, and elsewhere. Indeed, given the Ottoman resistance to education in Albanian, precisely in order to prevent the emergence of an idea of nationhood, these communities abroad were to provide the intellects who were to help shape Albanian nationalism in the twilight years of empire.

In 1878, when Serbia and Montenegro gained international recognition as independent states (though of course within smaller boundaries than today), the need for an assertion of Albanian nationalism was clear—not, as in the Serbian or Greek cases, against the Ottomans but rather as a defense against Serbian and Greek expansionism, which aimed to drive the Turks out of Europe and seize as much of the empire there, including Albanian-inhabited land, as they could. For Serbia the aim was to take as much of Macedonia as possible and, in its eyes, to liberate Kosovo, the holy places of the Serbian nation there, and parts of what are today Albania. Montenegrins, too, looked to Kosovo and also to northern Albania and especially Shkodër, which Montenegrins had long coveted as Skadar, a town that held an important place in legend, epic poetry, and their history.

So the role of Albanian nationalism was, as described in the wake of Albania's independence in 1912 by Mithat Frashëri, one of its founding fathers, to turn its people, "from a scattered array of clans into a nation." Until then Albanians had, in the words of Fatos Lubonja, an Albanian journalist and intellectual, only "identified themselves within the limits of their village, region or *bajrak* and recognised to some extent, the central government in Constantinople, or its representatives in the provinces, but they had very few spiritual, economic or intellectual ties with one another."[13] The task would not be easy given the lack of roads and communications to connect

Albanians and especially, in the wake of the Balkan wars of 1912 and 1913, when Kosovo and the other Albanian-inhabited lands in Montenegro and Macedonia were lost to the Serbs and Montenegrins. After that, Albanians were destined to live in different countries, and this would mark them in very different ways.

2

SERBS

Throughout history the map of Serbia has grown, shrunk, disappeared, and reappeared—several times. Sometimes Kosovo has been part of Serbia, sometimes not. Let's look at the last hundred years: In 1912 Serbian forces retook Kosovo from the Ottomans. In 1915 they lost it, only to return it again in 1918. But then Serbia itself disappeared from the map, dissolved into the new Kingdom of Serbs, Croats, and Slovenes, which in 1929 was officially renamed Yugoslavia, "the land of the South Slavs." In 1941 this state was wiped out by the Nazis and Mussolini's Italy. Most, but not all, of Kosovo became part of a Fascist Italian Greater Albania while Serbia reemerged, albeit as an occupied quisling state.

After the war Yugoslavia was re-created, this time as a federation of six republics of which Serbia was the largest, and Kosovo was destined to be its province. When that Yugoslavia was destroyed, drowned in blood in the wars of the 1990s, the Yugoslav name lingered until 2003, when it was replaced by the so-called state-union of Serbia and Montenegro, which in turn dissolved when the latter declared independence in June 2006. Finally, Serbia had returned to the map as independent state, but not by choice. All of its partners in the Yugoslav adventure, which began in 1918 and was tried again in the wake of the Second World War by the communist, Partisan leader Josip Broz Tito, had abandoned it. Serbia was once again alone, just as it had been on the eve of the First World War, but not by choice—by default.

But where were its borders? How far did its authority stretch? How far should it stretch and where were the Serbs? These were the questions that bedeviled the dying Yugoslavia and for which the wars of the 1990s were fought, not just on the battlefield but in words and argument too. For example, argued its politicians, academics, and diplomats, Kosovo should remain in Serbia, because it was legally part of the Serbian state and historically Serbian. By contrast, they said, the brief-lived Serbian breakaway state of Krajina in Croatia should not be part of Croatia but rather a part of the Greater Serbia that they eventually hoped to create, not just on the ground, as during the early 1990s during the war, but legally, too, because the majority of its people were Serbs.[1]

But where were the Serbs, in the past, and where are they now? As with the Albanians, it would be wrong and misleading to talk only of the Serbs of Kosovo. They are simply a very small part of a much bigger nation. To make sense of the Kosovo story, one has to see the bigger picture. The Serbs, even more so than the boundaries of Serbia, have moved, shifted, fled, and migrated through the centuries, in and out of Kosovo, and across the former Yugoslav space.

According to the 2002 census Serbia's population was just under 7.5 million, not including Kosovo. Of that number 82.8 percent were Serbs. In Bosnia there are estimated to be some 1.4 million Serbs, about 37 percent of the population, and in Croatia about 200,000 or 4.5 percent. In Montenegro, according to the 2003 census 198,414, or 32 percent, declared themselves to be Serbs, as did 35,939 or 1.78 percent in Macedonia.[2]

The wars of the 1990s sent hundreds of thousands of people fleeing. Some 600,000 Serbs were estimated to have ended up as refugees from Bosnia and Croatia in Serbia. On the eve of Kosovo's independence there were anywhere between 100,000 and 130,000 Serbs in Kosovo, but that number has fluctuated. I will examine this question later, along with the widely quoted—and most likely wrong—estimation that in the wake of Serbia's loss of control of Kosovo in 1999, some 230,000 people, mostly Serbs but including some Roma, fled the province.

Over the centuries Serbs have been in constant movement. For example, when the Ottomans arrived in Kosovo in the 14th century, most scholars, unless they are Albanians, seem to agree that the majority of the population were Serbs, or at least an Orthodox Christian population that would later identify themselves collectively as Serbs. Over the centuries, as we shall see in the next chapter, this was to change, as Serbs migrated to what are today Serbia, Hungary, Bosnia, and Croatia. For much of the Ottoman period towns in Serbia and Bosnia were Turkish and Muslim-dominated, with Christians living as peasants in the surrounding countryside. As Serbia began to emerge from Ottoman domination, beginning with the first Serbian uprising of 1804, then as a principality still owing loyalty to the sultan, and then, after 1878, as a recognized and fully independent state, Serbs were increasingly attracted to live there and indeed given land and encouraged to migrate from the still Ottoman-dominated parts such as Kosovo. Going the other way were Muslims, Turks, and Albanians, who either chose to leave or were forced to flee, as in the case of the Albanians from the areas around Niš and Valjevo, which Serbia took in 1878. Many headed for Kosovo.

The wars of the 20th century, that is, the Balkan Wars of 1912 and 1913, the two World Wars, and then the wars of the 1990s, also displaced millions upon millions, depositing Serbs and their neighbors where they are today. This includes large numbers abroad, many for example who fled at the end of the Second World War, either because they had fought on the losing side or because they did not want to live under communism.

But war was not the only factor that compelled people to move. In the Yugoslav period huge numbers migrated in different directions, too. Serbs and Montenegrins were invited to settle in Kosovo after 1918. During the communist years Serbs also migrated from Kosovo and Bosnia and other poorer parts of Yugoslavia, and were invited to settle the fertile farmlands of Vojvodina, in northern Serbia, following the expulsion and flight of its historic German population and many of its Hungarians, too. Attracted by the jobs, people came to work and settle in the big industrial cities. For education, the brightest and best went to Belgrade University above all, and especially if they came from Kosovo, they were unlikely to return to their backward province afterward. This phenomenon was not unique to Serbs. Croats from outside Croatia gravitated to it, Muslims from Sandžak, that strip of land shared between Serbia and Montenegro, to Bosnia, and many Yugoslav Albanians from Macedonia and Montenegro to Kosovo, especially once Pristina's university had been established as a fully fledged Albanian-language institution in 1969.

Serbs, like other Yugoslavs, also moved abroad in large numbers to work during the communist era, especially as *gastarbeiters* (guest workers) in Germany, Austria, Switzerland, Scandinavia, and elsewhere. Since the end of Yugoslavia hundreds of thousands have also left the region, both as refugees and as migrants seeking a better life elsewhere. In 2007 there were estimated to be more than 700,000 Serbs in Germany and 1.8 million Serbs—or at least people of Serbian descent—in the United States, and more than 750,000 in Canada. Among them are some of Serbia's best brains, keen to get away from a country and region unable as yet to fully realize its potential and break free of the past.

This bodes ill for the future of Serbia and the Serbs. While Serbia's leaders have concentrated much of their political capital on Kosovo in recent years, their country's population has been falling, despite the influx of refugees. Today, according to Božidar Djelić, Serbia's deputy prime minister in 2007, his country is losing 25,000 to 30,000 people a year, or 0.3 percent of its population. Serbia, he notes, is the fourth-oldest nation in the world, with an average age of 40.2. Although the birth rate has risen slightly since the fall in 2000 of Slobodan Milošević, Serbia's wartime leader, Serbia is still at the bottom of the list of European countries, with fewer than one child per marriage, that is, far less than the 2.1 required.[3]

Serbia is not alone in this, however. This is a general problem in all of the former Yugoslav states, except for one: Kosovo, whose population is among the youngest in Europe. Oddly, the demographic question, one which posed the issue of Kosovo within an aging Serbia and in terms of whether it would be good for Serbia and the Serbs to retain this young, growing, and ferociously hostile population within their state was one that was asked, but only rarely.

Historically, one question that has been asked is: "What makes a Serb a Serb?" Academics love to discuss what makes a nation a nation. Is it language, religion, a common culture, history, or what? And, for every definition there will always be exceptions, for example the Swiss, who are definitely a nation but have no common religion or language. With the Albanians, we have seen that it was language that served as the single most important factor that united them, since religion could not.

History molded the Serbian nation differently. Being Serb today derives from being Orthodox. The two things are intertwined, even if one is not in the slightest religious. Of course there are always oddities and small variations on the theme. For example you can be Serbian and Jewish, and in the past there have been Serbian Catholics and Croatian Orthodox, but, in the main, these are odd exceptions to the rule. Religion has made the Slavs of southeastern Europe what they are. Catholic Slavs in the region of the former Yugoslavia became Slovenes or Croats; Orthodox became Serbs and some of them, more recently, Macedonians and Montenegrins; Muslims, until the 1990s, were just "Muslims" and defined as such. Now, more often than not, they are called Bosniaks, even if, as in the case of Bosniaks in Kosovo, their ancestors always lived there, and not in Bosnia.

3
CREATING HISTORY

Every nation has a story, its myths about history and ancestry. In the Serbian story Kosovo looms large. Serbs like to hark back to the Middle Ages as a high point in their past and thus common identity. Before, there were only disparate lords and peasants. After, centuries of Ottoman domination. A glorious past was thus the hope of a glorious future and in that story Kosovo was to become central, especially as Serbs began, after their first rebellion of 1804 against the Ottomans, to re-create a state, looking to the past for inspiration. To understand this, we need to understand why Serbs say that Kosovo is the cradle of their civilization and their Jerusalem.

The Serbs, as Slavs, began to arrive in waves of migration from the middle of the sixth century A.D. Albanians claim descent from the tribes that inhabited the region before the Romans. The "who was there first" argument has long been fought in the trenches of academia. The Albanians say they were in Kosovo first, as Illyrians and Dardanians, and thus have the right of first ownership, and that the Slavs invaded their land. Serbs say that while there might have been some Albanians in Kosovo during the Middle Ages, the vast majority of the population was Serb, that Kosovo was at the center of their medieval kingdom, and that this only began to change after the arrival of the Ottomans when Albanians began to migrate into what is now Kosovo from what is now Albania. They also point out that the majority of the toponyms in Kosovo, including the name Kosovo itself, have Slavic roots.

The Serbian churches and monasteries of Kosovo, the Patriarchate of Peć/Peja, Dečani/Deçan, and Gračanica/Graçanica being the most notable of them, all testify to the legacy of the Nemanjić Dynasty, which did so much to shape the history of the Serbs and played such a crucial role in forging a people who until then were but a collection of tribes, feudal lords, and princes. Stefan Nemanja was the founder of the Serbian royal dynasty. He was born in 1109 in what is now Montenegro, the scion of a noble family from Raška, which today is often called by its Turkish name, Sandžak. By the time of his abdication in 1196 he ruled most of what is now Montenegro, Hercegovina, and much of Kosovo and of central Serbia.

Nemanja founded more than a dynasty. He began the tradition of Serbian royals building churches and monasteries. The link with the church was far more profound than this. Influenced by his third son, Rastko, known today as St. Sava, he gave up his throne to become a monk. Sava's legacy survives to this day. In 1219 he secured autocephaly (autonomy) for the Serbian church. He was thus the founder of the Serbian Orthodox Church, initially centered in Žiča in Sandžak but later moved to Peć, in Kosovo.

The 13th century was one of expansion and consolidation for the Nemanjićs and their feudal Serbian state. Much of this was thanks to the mineral wealth of their lands, not least the mines of Novo Brdo/Novobërda in central Kosovo. On Easter Sunday in 1346, Tsar Dušan had himself crowned the "Emperor of the Serbs and the Greeks" in Skopje. Later he added the Albanians and the Bulgars to his subjects. His imperial rule extended from Belgrade to Dubrovnik to Thessalonika, to all of Albania and into modern-day Bulgaria. In 1355, when Dušan died, his forces were threatening Constantinople itself. With his death the empire began to dissolve. Soon the enemy were no longer the Byzantines, as they had been, but the Ottoman Turks. By the time of the famous Battle of Kosovo, at Kosovo Polje/Fushë Kosova—the "Field of Blackbirds"—on June 28, 1389, Dušan's empire was no more and Serbian nobles were quarreling among themselves. The hero of the battle is Lazar, born around 1329, near Novo Brdo, who had married a woman from a junior branch of the Nemanjić family.

Surprisingly little is known about this famous battle. We know that Lazar died, as did the Ottoman sultan Murad. On the Serbian side were Bosnians and most probably some Albanians. Whether Lazar was really betrayed by Vuk Branković, one of his allies, is uncertain, as is the tale that Murad was murdered by Miloš Obilić, who was pretending to surrender to him. The first reports to spread across Europe spoke of a Serbian victory. Only later were these to be corrected.

While the battle is now remembered as a grand defeat, in purely military terms it was something of a draw. However, the Ottoman Turks had far more wealth, manpower, and reserves to call upon in the decades that followed. Bayezid, Murad's son, secured his succession and then returned to make Serbia into a vassal state. This meant that Lazar's son Stefan could succeed him but had to pay tribute and fight alongside Bayezid. Stefan's sister Olivera was sent to Bayezid's harem. In the decades that followed, Serbia slipped in and out of Ottoman control but by 1459 was under full Ottoman rule.

How does this help explain the present? The answer is that over the centuries the story made Kosovo under the Nemanjićs a central part of the Serbian narrative, particularly beginning in the 19th century. Two elements are crucial here. One is the role of the church. What Sava and the Nemanjićs had done was twofold. First, they firmly anchored the Serbs in the Orthodox world. Before that they had teetered between Catholic Rome and Constantinople. Second, they built the Nemanjić state on two pillars: the medieval state and the church. When the state was swept away by the Ottomans, the church continued to exist, and with most of the Nemanjićs canonized and staring down from the walls of their frescoed churches upon generation after generation, the belief was sustained that what was could be again.

The other element is the role played by Serbian epic poems that were sung around the hearth for hundreds of years. Just as Serbia's medieval kings were preserved in paint, stories of a heroic past were preserved in song. Many concerned Lazar, and some may have been the medieval version of propaganda. His widow, Milica, wanted to build Lazar's story into myth in order to bolster Stefan's claim to the throne. True or not, these epics preserved the Kosovo story through the ages. In the 19th century, they were transcribed by Vuk Karadžić, the famous Serbian linguist, who thus provided a written narrative for the emerging Serbian middle class, feeding their appetite for a national identity. This is the most famous poem of them all, "The Downfall of the Serbian Empire." Sultan Murad is advancing on Kosovo and Lazar is summoned to make his fateful choice:

> Flying hawk, grey bird,
> out of the holy place, out of Jerusalem,

holding a swallow, holding a bird,
that is Elijah, holy one;
holding no swallow, no bird,
but writing from the Mother of God
to the Emperor at Kosovo.
He drops that writing on his knee,
it is speaking to the Emperor:
"Lazar, glorious Emperor,
which is the empire of your choice?
Is it the empire of heaven?
Is it the empire of the earth?
If it is the empire of the earth,
saddle horses and tighten girth-straps,
and, fighting men, buckle on swords,
attack the Turks,
and all the Turkish army shall die.
But if the empire of heaven
weave a church on Kosovo,
build its foundations not with marble stones,
build it with pure silk and with crimson cloth,
take the Sacrament, marshal the men,
they shall die,
and you shall die among them as they die."
And when the Emperor heard those words,
He considered and thought,
"King God, what shall I do, how shall I do it?
Is it the empire of heaven?
Is it the empire of the earth?
And if I shall chose the empire,
and choose the empire of the earth,
the empire of earth is brief,
heaven is everlasting."

And the emperor chose the empire of heaven
Above the empire of the earth.[1]

The idea is simple. Serbs would rather die honorably than live
as vassals. But the Lazar story, replete with his Christlike last
supper before the battle, also contains within it the story of
resurrection. As Christ would be resurrected, so would Serbia.
On the 500th anniversary of the battle, in 1889, Čedomil
Mijatović, Serbia's foreign minister, said that

> an inexhaustible source of national pride was discovered on
> [sic] Kosovo. More important than language and stronger than
> the Church, this pride unites all Serbs in a single nation.... The
> glory of the Kosovo heroes shone like a radiant star in the dark
> night of almost five hundred years.... There was never a war
> for freedom—and when was there no war?—in which the
> spirit of Kosovo heroes did not participate. The new history of
> Serbia begins with Kosovo—a history of valiant efforts, long
> suffering, endless wars, and unquenchable glory.... We bless
> Kosovo because the memory of the Kosovo heroes upheld us,
> encouraged us, taught us and guided us.[2]

In 1889 Kosovo was still part of the Ottoman Empire but
Mijatović's rhetoric established a direct link between the new
Serbian state, recognized in 1878 at the Congress of Berlin,
with its medieval predecessor. But more was at stake here. As
Jean-Arnault Dérens points out, the 1889 commemoration was
also an occasion at which the new state reconciled with the
Serbian Orthodox Church, which had played no significant
role in the progressive liberation of Serbia from the Turks that
began in 1804. From then on, argues Dérens, the church began
to make of Kosovo "a mystical space," a symbol of resistance

to secularization and modernization, and later to the Albanian demographic threat. After 1945, it was a symbol of resistance to communism itself.[3] Dérens argues that two 20th-century Serbian theologians, Nikolaj Velimirović and Justin Popović, helped to nourish the idea of the Serbs as a "heavenly people," "a new chosen people, because of the suffering they had endured." In this way, points out Dérens, if all of the Serbs left Kosovo and all of its churches there were destroyed, Kosovo would remain the Serbian Jerusalem. And "Jerusalem could be lost, without the spiritual and historical significance of this city being altered."[4]

Most Albanians regard most Serbs' view about Kosovo's history and significance as so much bunk. Lenard Cohen, who has written a biography of Slobodan Milošević, quotes Ismail Kadare, Albania's best-known living writer. It is worth recording here what Kadare says because he faithfully reflects the Albanian view of Kosovo's story:

> Any discussion on Kosovo today begins with the cliché: "sacred territory for the Serbs"; the "cradle of the Serbian nation." … The core of [Serb] mythology goes as follows: at the time of the Battle in 1389, the Serbs were a majority in a region that was at the heart of their Kingdom; the Albanians only came into the territory after the Battle. This is a crude distortion and its effect in any public discussion on TV or elsewhere is to preempt any Albanian from putting across a different view or attempting some clarification of history. … The Battle of Kosovo was not a confrontation solely between Serbs and Turks. It was a battle fought by all the people of the Balkans united against an invader. All the histories list the names of the Balkan peoples who fought alongside one another against a common disaster: Serbs, Bosnians, Albanians and

Romanians....The Battle which should have been preserved
in memory as a symbol of friendship between the Balkan
peoples, was appropriated by criminal Serbs to serve their
purposes.[5]

In the end, in the Balkans or elsewhere, what matters is
not historical truth but what people believe it to be. Today
statues of Serbian kings and heroes in Albanian-controlled
parts of Kosovo have disappeared, to be replaced by Albanian
ones. Streets once dedicated to communist heroes and then
Serbian ones have now been renamed for Albanian ones. In
the center of Pristina Albanians have erected an equestrian
statue of Skanderbeg, the Albanian medieval hero. It is similar
to the one that dominates Tirana's central square, which is
also named after him, and which replaced the statue of Stalin
in 1961—after Enver Hoxha's communist dictatorship broke
with the Soviet Union.

Just as Lazar and the Nemanjićs provide the historical
backbone for Serbian history, Skanderbeg has come to do the
same for Albanians: a medieval hero with whom they all can
identify. He is, however, as the Albanian journalist and writer
Fatos Lubonja points out, a "very ambivalent figure."[6] Born
Gjergj Katriot in 1403, he was the son of an Albanian noble
subdued by the Ottomans and sent to Istanbul as a hostage.
There he was converted to Islam, fought alongside the sultan,
and took the name Skanderbeg, from the Turkish *Iskender Bey*,
"Lord Alexander."

In 1443, however, back in Albania, Skanderbeg turned
against the Turks, converted back to Christianity, and liber-
ated large parts of what is today Albania. Skanderbeg, the
Muslim apostate, is "ambivalent" of course because by the
time he was championed in the 19th century as the national

hero par excellence, most Albanians were Muslims. Over the years, Skanderbeg both allied with Serbian princes and fought against them. His daughter was married to one, which proves that we must be careful in projecting the politics and history of the present back into the distant past. Just as Kosovo became an idea that helped inspire the romantic nationalism of 19th-century Serbia, Skanderbeg was a convenient hero. He fitted the ideal discussed earlier, that religion did not define what it meant to be Albanian. As Lubonja points out, when Albanians were looking "for a big brother who would replace Turkey in defending them from the Serbian and Greek threat...the 'Champion of Christianity' was a most appropriate hero because he was also a hero of the Christian Western world."[7] The noted Albanian publisher and writer Piro Misha says that Skanderbeg was the right man in the right place at the right time.

> As with most myths, his figure and his deeds became a mixture of historical facts, truths, half-truths, inventions and folklore. Skanderbeg was made a national hero although his action had never really involved all Albanians. Neither Kosovo nor most parts of the south were ever included.... Therefore, the figure of Skanderbeg needed some adjustment. In particular, his Christian orientation could damage the cause. In Arbëresh poems he was not only the defender of their home country, he was also the defender of Christianity.[8] For nineteenth-century Albanians, a majority of whom had adhered to the faith of Skanderbeg's Muslim enemies, this religious dimension needed to be avoided. Consequently, Skanderbeg became simply the national hero of Albanians, the embodiment of the myth of "continuous resistance" against their numerous foes over the centuries.[9]

Today, the Albanian flag, a red banner with a double-headed eagle, although derived from that of Byzantium, is believed to have its origins in the seal of Skanderbeg. His image is everywhere in Kosovo. And yet, curiously, Skanderbeg as a problematic hero, and the issue of Albanians as a people caught between East and West continues to be openly discussed. In 2007, Ismail Kadare engaged in a major polemical debate with Rexhep Qosja, a well-known Kosovo Albanian nationalist academic. Kadare argued that Albanians could and should deepen their links with Europe and even Catholicism by placing less emphasis on their Ottoman past and Islam. This idea was rejected by Qosja, who said that it was not possible to separate the Albanian identity from these elements of their history and tradition.

Tradition, of course, is not something static. I have already noted that the roles of Lazar and Skanderbeg have varied in relation to the demands of the times. Two other elements of the Kosovo Albanian past bear mention. The first relates to Adem Jashari and the creation of a new national icon for Kosovo Albanians, if not all Albanians. Jashari was the bushy-bearded hero of the Kosovo Liberation Army (KLA) whose death in Prekaz along with those of his family and others in 1998 at the hands of the Serbs sparked the 1999 Kosovo War. His image has become ubiquitous in Kosovo, his house a shrine, and the field where he and the family are buried a place of pilgrimage. Jashari is becoming a modern-day Skanderbeg and embodiment of what Misha calls above "continuous resistance." Anna Di Lellio and Stephanie Schwandner-Sievers, scholars who have written about the phenomenon, have noted that his story has become a "founding myth" for Kosovo, "like the siege and battle of the Alamo in Texas in 1836," which ended with the death of Davy Crockett. The story of Prekaz, they write, "provides a very powerful narration and link to memory."

> The protagonists were killed but are not represented as vanquished; they are not considered victims, but as heroes who knew no surrender. They are in fact called *dëshmorët e kombit* (martyrs of the nation), which is not the same as *shahid* (Islamic martyr of Jihad), although the Jasharis, like the overwhelming majority of Albanians in Kosovo are Muslim. They are martyrs in the original sense of "witness to the cause" as present in Christian and Islamic theologies: although nationhood is denied them, they testify with their martyrdom that the nation does exist.[10]

Interestingly, the Jasharis are buried in a field called the "field of peace." It was here in the early 1990s that rituals of reconciliation took place for families embroiled in blood feuds.[11] These were inspired by Anton Çetta, a retired professor and folklore scholar who had led a campaign to end such vendettas, which had begun to reassert themselves in Kosovo with the end of communism. Tradition holds that these feuds are rooted in the 15th-century *Kanun* or Canon of Lek Dukagjini, which enshrined the principle of blood vengeance.

Codes upholding family honor and regulating conduct between families and people is nothing specific to Albanians, and indeed was widespread in both the Ottoman world and in places such as Sicily, southern Italy, and Corsica. The reemergence of *Kanun*, in northern Albania and to a certain extent in Kosovo with the end of communism, suggests Albanians were looking for a source of authority when the law of the land could no longer perform its function. Çetta's campaign, too, should also be seen in the context of a need to keep Albanians ⟩ united at a time when the common enemy was Serbia.

Today, *Kanun* is seen as an important part of Kosovo's Albanian heritage, although also something that most urbanites and educated people would prefer consigned to the history books, because it points to the failure of Kosovo to make a modern state. When blood feuds again appeared in Kosovo this was indeed "a consequence of the poor functioning of law and order and the institutions that regulate the law," according to Pajazit Nushi, a human rights activist whose organization had recorded some 40 blood feud–related murders from 1999 to 2003.[12] While Albanians believe that *Kanun* finds its roots in the code developed by an Albanian prince and contemporary of Skanderbeg, Stephanie Schwandner-Sievers, one of the world's leading experts in Albanian anthropology, posits another theory: that in fact it reaches back to antiquity and that its name is possibly an Albanianization of the *Lex Duodecim Tabularum*, the foundation of Roman law. She also notes, however, that today *Kanun* has taken on another significance, above and beyond its original one. Among Albanians, she asserts, it has "become part of the canon of their identity."

4

FROM DARDANIA TO YUGOSLAVIA

For as long as anyone can remember, the history of Kosovo has been a battlefield pitting Serbs against Albanians. Each believes different things because each has been taught different things, and as they reach further back into time it becomes easier to argue whatever they want in order to find support for their view of the present. This quarrel is best illustrated in the issue of Kosovo's name.

Historically and geographically, the region now circumscribed by the borders drawn after the Second World War encompasses two regions. To the east is Kosovo proper and to the west, bounded by the dramatic mountains that divide it from Albania and Montenegro, is the plain known by Serbs as Metohija and by Albanians as Rrafsh i Dukagjinit, "the Dukagjin plateau." The towns of Peć/Peja, Djakovica/Gjakova, and Prizren lie in the latter while Mitrovica, Pristina, and Uroševac/Ferizaj lie in Kosovo. The word "Metohija" derives from the Greek for church or monastic lands. Close to Peć is the historical home of the Serbian Orthodox Patriarchate, and nearby Visoki Dečani is one of the greatest and most beautiful churches of all of southeastern Europe. The name "Dukagjin" is believed to derive from a medieval Albanian noble family.

"Kosovo" itself comes from the Serbian word _Kos_, which means blackbird. During most of the communist period and indeed today, as far as Serbian officials are concerned, Kosovo was and is known as Kosovo and Metohija, sometimes shortened to Kosmet. It is a name never used by Albanians. "Metohija" links its past (and thus present) to that of the Serbian Orthodox Church, while to call it Kosovo, or Kosova in Albanian, emphasizes its unity as one territory.

But even this is not without controversy, given the Slavic origin of the name. After all, if the root of Kosovo's name is Slav, then that would seem to contradict the Albanian argument that they had lived here before the Serbs and thus that Kosovo belongs to them. This was a point with which Ibrahim Rugova, the Kosovo Albanian leader who died in January 2006, had considerable sympathy. He thus toyed with the idea of renaming Kosovo "Dardania," after the ancient Illyrian tribe supposed to have lived in Kosovo in antiquity. Hence while the official flag of the president of Kosovo has at its center Skanderbeg's double-headed eagle it also has the name Dardania emblazoned across it. For some time a banner celebrating Rugova hung from a ministry building in Pristina with a picture of Rugova and a declaration commemorating him as president of Dardania. As far as partisans of Dardania are concerned this theory has an added historical cum political advantage. They argue that the ancient Dardanians were the ancestors of the Albanians but more important in this context, Roman Catholics. Thus, they argue, Albanians were historically part of Western civilization and their churches were usurped and turned into Orthodox ones by the invading Slavs, who were not.

The latter is not a view that has fallen on fertile ground outside of Albanian circles. In general terms historians believe that Serbs, or at least the people who would later identify themselves as such, were by far the majority in Kosovo until the Ottoman conquest, and that after that this began to change, albeit very slowly over the centuries. Conversion also played its part. Some Serbs converted to Islam under the Turks; some became Albanianized, too. By contrast, a far higher proportion of Albanians converted to Islam, perhaps because they did not have a national church like the Serbs, and Catholicism was not so deeply entrenched among them as it was, say, among Croats. Conversions, however, do not explain the major demographic shifts that were to take place in Kosovo and the region, especially after the Ottomans consolidated their control of Serbia after the fall of Smederevo in 1459. After this, the authority of the Peć Patriarchate was abolished and its authority transferred to Greek-speaking bishops in Ohrid, in Macedonia. In the centuries that followed, the Serbian and Orthodox population gradually shifted northward, to Hungary, to what is today Vojvodina, and to Bosnia, Dalmatia, and Croatia.

Two key dates need concern us here. The first is 1557 when the Patriarchate in Peć was restored thanks to the intervention of Mehmed Sokollu, grand vizier to Suleiman the Magnificent. Sokollu was born Sokolović, a Bosnian Serb, and the first patriarch was Makarije, a member of the Sokolović clan. The effect of this act reverberates through history to this day. The church as the spiritual guardian of the Serbian nation was reborn and rejuvenated. Churches in Kosovo and elsewhere were restored and the memory of the Nemanjić era hallowed. Had this not happened, had the church not been allowed to revive and to preserve "Serbdom" over the centuries, the history of Kosovo and the region would doubtless have been very different. Contrast the Serbian experience with Bosnia, where, lacking

such a church and institutions, many Slavs converted to Islam
in the wake of the conquest in 1463, thus eventually giving
birth to the nation that identifies itself today as Bosniak, or
Bosnian Muslim.

The second key date is 1690. Almost three hundred years after
Lazar's Battle of Kosovo, the Ottoman advance was finally
halted at the siege of Vienna in 1683. After that Habsburg
forces began to reverse the Turkish tide. In 1688 Belgrade was
taken, and forces led by Count Eneo Piccolomini swept south
to Kosovo and to Skopje. Serbs and Catholic Albanians were
called upon to rise up and throw off the Ottoman yoke. Many
did. Then disaster struck. On January 2, 1690, the Austrians
were defeated in battle at the Kačanik/Kaçanik gorge
through which the road runs from Kosovo to Macedonia.
Ottoman vengeance was swift and terrible, and in the wake
of the defeat the Habsburg emperor invited the Serbian patriarch, Arsenije III, to lead his people to safety. This has gone
down as the "Great Migration." Tens of thousands of Serbs
are thought to have left with him, to settle in regions that
would become the militarized frontier between Habsburg
and Ottoman territories, in those parts of modern Croatia
and Vojvodina that were then the borderlands with Ottoman
Bosnia and Serbia.

In this way, runs the most widely accepted view, Kosovo's
demography began to change, as this and further migrations,
into which were included Albanian Catholics, led to parts
of Kosovo becoming depopulated. The Ottomans were to
encourage resettlement here with loyal Albanian Muslims,
many of whom were now to come down from the mountains of Albania to the fertile plains of Kosovo or to western
Macedonia.

Unfortunately, this being Kosovo, the seminal event that is said to have led to the beginning of its great population shifts does not, unsurprisingly, go unchallenged. Noel Malcolm, the British historian who wrote an important history of Kosovo, argues that his research in European archives leads him to conclude that much of the story of the "Great Migration" is actually false. He argues that the situation was far more confused—some Serbs or Orthodox refused to rise up, some fought on the Ottoman side, and many Albanians, including some Muslims, fought on the Austrian side. He notes that Prizren, where a key part of the story took place, was also, by then, already an overwhelmingly Albanian and Muslim town. When the end came, he says, there was no invitation to the patriarch as such, and thus he did not lead a migration, but rather caught up with refugees heading north, the majority of whom did not, Malcolm believes, come from Kosovo at all, but from central Serbia.[1] Such are the vicissitudes of history. Even with regard to such a key event in Kosovo's history, there is no agreement.

The 18th and 19th centuries were ones in which Kosovo was periodically racked by revolt and war, interspersed with years of relative peace. In 1766 the Peć Patriarchate was abolished and the center of Serbian Orthodoxy shifted northward to Sremski Karlovci in Habsburg Vojvodina. The 18th century saw an increased pace of conversion to Islam in the region, more commonly as we have noted among Albanians than Serbs.

The vast majority of people in Kosovo were peasants but power lay with the Muslim Albanian aristocracy. As Muslims, Albanians could and did rise to the highest positions in the Ottoman Empire. They came to have ambivalent feelings toward it, especially as the empire went into decline. The reason was paradoxical. To stem the decline the empire tried to reform, but the problem, as far as Albanians were concerned, was that these reforms actually interfered in the way they had always run things at home. The 1840s, for example, were years of upheaval as Kosovo Albanian *beys*, lords or leaders, revolted against the so-called *Tanzimat* reforms of Istanbul, which attempted to rein in their power. Decline also meant that Albanians were forced to confront their future, which now came face to face with the reemergence of the Balkan Christian states beginning with the Serbian revolt of 1804.

As noted, the Albanians came late to the nationalist struggles of the Balkans. However, as Serbia, Greece, Montenegro, and Bulgaria all began to return to the map of Europe, Albanians realized that unless they organized themselves, their lands and future would be threatened. At first their response was to demand autonomy within the empire, and 1878 is the key date here. This was the year that saw Serbia expanding southward and taking Niš. The Albanian quarter was burned and Albanians from the surrounding villages forced to flee. Albanians from several other towns and regions, such as Toplica, Vranje, Leskovac, and Prokuplje suffered the same fate. The Serbian-Turkish wars of 1876–1878 caused massive dislocations, with hundreds of thousands put to flight in all directions. Some 50,000 now came to settle in Kosovo, most of them Albanian. Some Slav Muslims came from Montenegro and some from Bosnia, which was now occupied by the Austro-Hungarians. In this climate, and given that Serbia and Montenegro were recognized as fully independent (as opposed to autonomous provinces of the empire) at the Congress of Berlin, thousands of Serbs also left Kosovo. In fact, Serbs had over the past few generations already been moving to the Serbian principality, which had been eager to bolster its

population, and giving land to peasants to attract them. Now
people went for a mix of reasons, as they have done ever since.
At this point, during and just after the war, some left in fear
of their lives as Albanian gangs or semi-official units raided
villages, and some were attracted by the opportunities offered
by life in the new, expanding, and confident state.

The Albanian response of 1878 was the League of Prizren.
It was the first blow for Albanian nationalism, albeit clearly a
defensive action. Fearing that unless they acted, their lands
would eventually be carved up by the other Balkan states,
including Bulgaria, Albanian leaders were called to Prizren
to decide on the best course of action. At first, most of them
were from Kosovo and most of them Muslim. Some argued
for an autonomous Albanian state within the empire, some
emphasized the defense of Muslim traditions that they
feared were being threatened by modernizing reforms. A key
demand was for an Albanian *vilayet*, or region, be created
from the four existing ones that covered the main areas where
Albanians lived.

Initially, the League was not opposed by Istanbul, but by
1880, relations had deteriorated. Important voices were now
calling for the creation of an independent Albanian state
and the League, in effect, took over the running of Kosovo.
In 1881 it was crushed by Turkish troops. Its important
legacy however was that, for the first time, it was seen that
Albanians could actually work together for their common
national interest, something they had never done before.

It was high time for Albanians to think like this. Given
Serbia's southward expansion, by 1878 Kosovo was in its
sights and now an attainable objective. It also fell within the
vision of the Načertanije, or draft plan, of Ilija Garašanin, a
towering figure of Serbian 19th-century politics who argued

in favor of (re)claiming Macedonia and what was increasingly called "Old Serbia" (Kosovo and the Sandžak), to distinguish it from the new Serbian state. He argued that unless Serbia emerged as the strongest country in the Balkans as the Ottoman Empire collapsed, the void would be filled by small states dominated by Austro-Hungary and the Russians. The Austro-Hungarians, especially after their occupation of Bosnia in 1878, were keen to counter Serbian and local Slav nationalisms, because they were a threat to the empire. Thus they encouraged Albanian nationalism, hoping to create an Albanian state under their tutelage.

The years between 1878 and 1912, which saw the end of the Ottoman Empire in the Balkans, were—in Kosovo and Macedonia especially—ones of unrest, revolts, and instability. In 1908 the modernizing Young Turk revolution was initially welcomed by most in Kosovo, as in Albania, although few actually understood what it was about. After all, the idea of creating and consolidating an efficient and centralized Ottoman state of all of its citizens, regardless of religion, was not what most Albanians wanted, as opposed to preserving their powers and privileges at home, creating Albanian-language schools, and so on.

When the sultan was deposed the following year, Kosovo Albanians rose in revolt. Ottoman troops were, as usual, sent to quell the uprising, but until 1912 much of the province and increasingly much of Albania were to be in a state of more or less permanent revolt. Then, in August of that year, Istanbul conceded the demand for a unified Albania within the Ottoman Empire. It was too little, too late. In October, Montenegro, Serbia, and Bulgaria declared war, to be followed by Greece. In the midst of this, on November 28, Ismail Qemal, who had been an Albanian deputy in the Ottoman parliament, declared the independence of the Republic of Albania in the port town of Vlora. Ever since this has been celebrated by Albanians as their national day, known as Flag Day.

By the end of the fighting in 1912, Serbia had taken much of Kosovo, but Montenegro too was in possession of Peć/Peja, Dečani/Deçane, Djakovica/Gjakova, and much of the rest of the west. The Turks had been driven out, but parts of what was emerging as Albania proper were also occupied by the Serbs and by the Greeks in the south, and Shkodër/Skadar was in the hands of the Montenegrins. Greece took southern Macedonia including Thessalonika; Serbia took most of the rest, including the Albanian-inhabited parts. Bulgaria got a small portion in the east. The decisive battle for Kosovo took place in Kumanovo, now in northern Macedonia, on October 23 and 24.

In December 1912 a conference of ambassadors was convened in London. It was to decide that there should indeed be an Albanian state, more or less within the borders it has today, but in certain parts the actual line of the frontier needed to be settled. Thus, what constitutes Kosovo today was left divided between Serbia and Montenegro. Unsurprisingly, its Albanians were in revolt and, dissatisfied with its share of the Macedonian spoils, Bulgaria launched the second Balkan War in June 1913, in a failed attempt to take more.

Serbia, Montenegro, and Greece all had states and armies to mobilize, unlike the Albanians, so it is hardly surprising that they were unable to successfully resist in Kosovo. Indeed, if it had not been for Great Power politicking, it is possible that there would have been no Albania at all. The result of the wars and the territorial dispensation of 1913 came about thanks both to arms and as a compromise between Austro-Hungary, which wanted an Albanian state—in part to deny

Serbia access to the sea—and Russia, which wanted to help its Orthodox ally.

To this day, in different ways of course, all the same actors (or, for example, their descendants, in the case of Austro-Hungary) continue to play the same games in the region, while Albanians and Serbs and the other peoples and states of the Balkans continue to play them off against one another.

The Balkan Wars and now the First World War were absolutely devastating to the people of Kosovo and of course, the rest of the region. The Serbs naturally regarded the taking of Kosovo as a liberation, but by now only 30 or 40 percent of its population was still Serb. Albanians clearly regarded this as conquest, especially as for generations their leaders had been striving for the unification of all of the lands inhabited by Albanians. One Serbian solider wrote of the "indescribable excitement" of his unit as it halted on the battlefield of 1389. There the commander, with tears flowing down his cheeks, spoke to them saying, "The spirits of Lazar, Miloš [Obilić], and all the Kosovo martyrs gaze on us. We feel strong and proud, for we are the generation which will realize the centuries-old dream of the whole nation: that we with the sword will regain the freedom that was lost with the sword."[2]

Albanian resistance, led by men like Isa Boletin, who had been prominent in the revolt against the Young Turks, was crushed. Some 20,000 may have lost their lives and tens of thousands fled. Several appalling massacres took place, and the torching of one village was enough to set the inhabitants of the next in flight. According to the American Carnegie Endowment, which organized a visit to the region and which counted the editor of the *Economist* among its members, the aim of this was clear. "Houses and whole villages are reduced to ashes," it reported:

> unarmed and innocent populations massacred *en masse*, incredible acts of violence, pillage and brutality of every kind—such were the means which were employed and are still being employed by the Serbo-Montenegrin soldiery, with a view to the entire transformation of the ethnic character of the regions inhabited exclusively by Albanians.[3]

On June 28, 1914, Gavrilo Princip assassinated Archduke Franz Ferdinand, the heir to the Austro-Hungarian throne in Sarajevo. This was now the opportunity for the Dual Monarchy to crush Serbia and to realize its dreams of eventually taking Bosnia and even the other south Slav, or "Yugoslav," lands from it. With war declared, the Austro-Hungarians attacked, but to their amazement they found themselves repulsed by little Serbia. By 1915, however, the tide had turned and Serbia was invaded by them, along with the Germans and Bulgarians. Kosovo was divided between the Austro-Hungarians and the Bulgarians. Before their arrival, however, extraordinary scenes were witnessed. The Serbian government, king, army, and many more decided to evacuate the country. The only way out was across Kosovo, so huge columns tramped across it on their way to Montenegro and Albania. Their aim was to reach the Albanian coast in order to be rescued by the Allies. Tens of thousands were captured by the invading armies, and thousands died in the snow of the mountains. Many also died, picked off by Albanians eager for revenge for the carnage visited upon them in the last few years by the Serbs.

Once the Serbian soldiers reached the Albanian coast they were taken, beginning in January 1916, by French, British,

and Italian ships, first to Corfu. Many were to die there
from disease.[4] However, the survivors were eventually to
take their place alongside the Allied armies on the Salonika
(Thessalonika) Front. This act of heroism was to stand Serbia
in good stead. Its reputation was never higher, and Britain,
for example, was to celebrate "Kossovo Day" in 1916, and
the French collected funds to help the people of *la Serbie
martyre*.[5] Serbia was the little David standing up to the Austro-
Hungarian Goliath. It is hardly surprising, given that the
Kosovo Albanians had lost their chance to unite with Albania
and had been massacred by the Serbs in 1912 and 1913, that
they should welcome the new invaders. But of course, this was
to leave them on the wrong side of history at the end of the
war. There was some Kosovo Albanian resistance, especially
against the Bulgarians, but in October 1918 Serbian troops,
fighting alongside the French and Italians, returned.

On December 1, 1918, a new state, the Kingdom of
Serbs, Croats, and Slovenes, was declared. Informally it
was already called Yugoslavia. The kingdom, which took in
Croatia, Dalmatia, Vojvodina, Slovenia, Montenegro, Bosnia-
Hercegovina, Kosovo, and Macedonia, was dominated by
Serbia, as its core was the existing Serbian state, army, and
Karadjordjević monarchy. The biggest non-Slav minori-
ties were Germans and Hungarians in the north, mostly in
Vojvodina, and the Albanians, mostly in Kosovo.

5

KOSOVO IN YUGOSLAVIA

The reconquest was brutal. Serbian forces returning to Kosovo remembered the treatment they had received at the hands of Albanians during their retreat in 1915 and Albanians remembered their treatment at the hands of the Serbs in 1912 and 1913. Serbian troops, officially "Yugoslav" ones after December 1, 1918, were met with armed resistance by guerrilla cum bandit *kaçaks*. Just as the Serbs had been at war since 1912, many of these men had also been fighting for ten years or so. They had fought the Turks, the Serbs in the Balkan wars, then the Austro-Hungarians and Bulgarians, and now the Serbs again. Several thousand died and there were also several massacres of Albanians.[1]

Albanian armed resistance to their reincorporation into the Slav state lingered well into the 1920s, although it petered out significantly after 1924. It was supported by the Committee for the National Defence of Kosovo, which was set up in November 1918 in Shkodër, in northern Albania, by prominent Kosovo Albanian leaders, such as Hasan Prishtina. Known as the Kosovo Committee, or KK, its aim was to help and supply the *kaçaks*, not just in Kosovo but in Macedonia and Montenegro, too. Apart from Prishtina, the most prominent of its leaders were Bajram Curri and Azem Bejta. In 1919 the latter led up to 10,000 badly armed rebels in the central Drenica region. They were soon driven off by the army and bands of Serbs armed by the authorities. Azem Bejta was eventually killed in 1924, but his now even more famous wife, Shota Galica, carried on the struggle until her own death in 1927.

Two points need to be made here. One is that because the border with Albania had not been fully demarcated, a demilitarized zone had been created around the village of Junik. Just as was the case after 1999, when the demilitarized zone along the Kosovo and Serbian Preševo/Presheva border became a haven for Albanian guerrillas, this one did, too, and it was from here that many attacks were launched into Kosovo.

The end of significant *kaçak* resistance came, however, ✓ not simply because they were overwhelmed by the Serbs. A larger game was at stake. By 1920 Bajram Curri was Albania's minister of war, and in 1921 Hasan Prishtina became prime minister. But the Kosovars quickly fell into conflict with Ahmed Zogu (born "Zogolli," he subsequently changed his name to "Zog"), the country's minister of interior, who seized full power in 1922. Zog hit hard against his opponents and the KK, but the Kosovars and other opponents toppled him in 1924. The next year, however, supported by Yugoslav and refugee White Russian soldiers under their command, Zog returned to power in Tirana. Bajram Curri was killed. Zog now concentrated on consolidating his position and building a proper state in Albania. With the exception of the "Greater Albania" period during the Second World War, Zog's victory over the Kosovars in effect set Tirana's policy, which has been in place ever since: Albania, as opposed to Albanians, first. In 1928 he was crowned, albeit misleadingly, king of the Albanians, not of Albania.

Within Kosovo, a number of issues came to dominate the interwar years: education, Serbian colonists, and Albanian emigration. Schools have always played a major part in the Albanian story in Kosovo. The Turks had resisted schooling in Albanian because they were keen to prevent the emergence of an Albanian national identity. The Austrians, by contrast, keen to cultivate it, opened schools in Kosovo during their brief stay there during the First World War. These were soon shut down by the new Yugoslav authorities. (As we shall see, the issue of schools was to return to haunt Kosovo during the Milošević years.) Between the wars Albanian-language secular schools were banned. This was a restriction that did not apply to Yugoslavia's other two big minorities, the Germans and Hungarians. Schools were opened in Kosovo, but more in Serbian areas and where Serbs were being settled, and what schooling there was (less than a third of children went to school in Kosovo on the eve of the Second World War), was in Serbian. Muslim religious schools were not restricted. The theory of this, argues Denisa Kostovicova, who has studied the issue of *shkolla shqipe*, Albanian schools, was to "undermine the feeling of Albanian national identity by stimulating the supremacy of collective identification based on religion."[2] The policy was a complete failure. Underground schools developed, while in their schools "many Albanian *mullahs* began to stealthily teach 'national awakening' during religious classes, while Albanian students secretly circulated Albanian books in Serbian schools."[3]

The second troubling issue in this period is the question of Serbian colonists. The government in Belgrade was keen to change the demographics of Kosovo, especially given the hostility of the majority Albanians. Kosovo as such had disappeared from the map, however, divided between three new Yugoslav provinces. This was the fate of all of the new Yugoslavia, the authorities being keen to diminish old regional cum ethnic loyalties in a bid to create loyalty to something higher—that is, Yugoslavia itself.

In Kosovo colonization came hand in hand with land reform. Serbs and Montenegrins were given land confiscated from Albanians, former large landowners, or families of *kaçaks*. Officially anyone could benefit from the scheme but it was clearly skewed to favor Serbs. According to one estimate 14,000 families benefited, of whom 4,000 were Albanian. Some of those who took up the offer of land were families of those Serbs who had left after 1878, and others were Serbs and Montenegrins who had come from what was now the new Albanian state. In a curious antecedent to the house reconstruction aid that came to Kosovo after 1999, British and American charities helped build hundreds of houses.[4] Some new settler villages were given romantic names derived from the Serbian Kosovo epics, such as Obilić, close to Pristina, recalling Miloš Obilić, the man whom the epics say killed Sultan Murad in 1389.

As usual, exact figures are hard to come by. Estimates vary as to the number of colonists, but figures range up to 70,000. Some did not stay, however, either because of *kaçak* attacks or because, especially after 1929 and the Great Depression, they could not make a living through farming. In 1939 there were estimated to be 59,300 colonists in Kosovo, a figure that amounted to 9.3 percent of the population.[5]

At the same time that Serbs were coming to Kosovo, Albanians and Slav Muslims were leaving it as well as other parts of Yugoslavia, such as Macedonia. However, here the numbers are even more uncertain. Dozens of thousands, argue some; far more, argue others. The context was that Yugoslavia wanted to diminish the numbers of hostile or potentially hostile Albanians and Muslims, while Turkey wanted to repopulate regions of Anatolia emptied by the recent exodus of hundreds of thousands of Greeks and Turkish-speaking Christians. Between Greece and Turkey, this had been formalized by the 1923 Treaty of Lausanne, which saw the exchange of 1.3 million from Turkey and 350,000 Turks and Greek-speaking Muslims from Greece.

Some years later, in 1938 a convention foresaw the emigration of some 200,000 to Turkey from Yugoslavia, but it remained a dead letter thanks to the war. In 1937 Vaso Čubrilović, a historian at Belgrade University, who as a young man had taken part in the plot to kill the Archduke Franz Ferdinand in Sarajevo 1914, argued forcefully that the Albanians had to go. "The only way and the only means to cope with them is the brute force of an organised state...if we do not settle accounts with them at the proper time, within 20–30 years we shall have to cope with a terrible irredentism, the signs of which are already apparent and which will inevitably put all our southern territories in danger." Who would object to such a policy he argued, at a time "when Germany can expel tens of thousands of Jews and Russia can shift millions of people from one part of the continent to another"?[6]

For Yugoslavia the Second World War began later than in the West—on April 6, 1941, when Belgrade was bombed by the Nazis and the invasion of the country began. Resistance was feeble and rapidly collapsed. For Albanians as a nation, however, the war had begun early, indeed almost exactly two years to the day earlier, when, on April 7, 1939, Mussolini's Italy had invaded Albania. Resistance there had been even more feeble. Officially Albania retained a government, but it was to be bound to Italy in a personal union under King Victor

Emmanuel, who became king of Albania, too, replacing the deposed Zog, who had fled.

The Italian occupation was not popular, but one way to bolster it over the next two years was to encourage dreams of a Greater Albania. The collapse and division of Yugoslavia presented this opportunity. Kosovo was split into three. The Bulgarians were given part of the east and the Germans took a relatively large zone in the north. Not only did this take in Mitrovica and the Trepča/Trepça mines, but it stretched as far south as Vučitrn/Vushtrri. The rest, including western Macedonia, was now attached to what became known as "Old Albania." The creation of this Greater Albania was welcomed by most Kosovo Albanians. The northern, German sector was officially part of occupied Serbia, but in fact the Nazis installed an autonomous Albanian regime here, set up schools, and in general terms, and much to the annoyance of the Italians, allowed the Albanians more autonomy here than the Italians did in Greater Albania. They even tolerated some anti-Italian activities.[7] According to the historian Bernd Fischer, 40 percent of Germany's wartime lead demand was supplied by Trepça.[8]

In the chaos that followed the Yugoslav collapse, Kosovo Serbs were attacked and villages burned to the ground. As usual figures are hard to come by, and the number of those who fled or were expelled varies between 30,000 and 100,000, although 70,000 refugees from Kosovo had been registered in Belgrade by April 1942. Colonists were the first but not the only target of Albanian attacks. Many Serbs were sent to concentration camps in Pristina and Mitrovica. According to Fischer, these Serbs "were apparently used as labor on fortification works in Italian Albania and as workers in the Trepça mines for the Germans."[9]

In Albania itself resistance to the Italians and, after their collapse in September 1943, to the Germans who followed them, was growing. It came from both nationalist and Zogist groups, and also from the communists led by Enver Hoxha. Resistance in Kosovo was a different story. There the real enemy, as far as most Albanians were concerned, were the Serbs, and the Allies were making no promises about not returning Kosovo to Yugoslav control after the war. So, up to the end, the communists and Partisans there made little headway, also because its minuscule communist party membership had always been overwhelmingly Serb. In the wake of the Italian withdrawal, the Albanians demanded that the Germans attach the north to the rest of Kosovo and Greater Albania, but apart from some minor concessions, they refused. They did however consider Kosovo to be the ideal recruiting ground for an SS battalion, which was named for Skanderbeg. It proved to be unreliable, and according to Fischer, its men "gained an unenviable reputation, apparently preferring rape, pillage, and murder to fighting, particularly in Serbian areas."[10]

The meeting that laid the foundations for the new Yugoslavia, presided over by Josip Broz Tito in Jajce in Bosnia in 1943, did not include any Kosovo Albanian delegates. By contrast, at a meeting in Bujan in northern Albania over the New Year of 1943–1944, a key declaration was made: "Kosovo-Metohija is an area with a majority Albanian population, which, now as always in the past, wishes to be united with Albania." It continued:

> The only way that the Albanians of Kosovo-Metohija can be united with Albania is through a common struggle with the other peoples of Yugoslavia against the occupiers and their

lackeys. For the only way freedom can be achieved is if all peoples, including the Albanians, have the possibility of deciding their own destiny, with the right to self-determination, up to and including secession.[11]

Those Kosovo Albanians that did fight for the Partisans now clearly expected that after the war Kosovo would remain united with Albania. It was, of course, not to be. As the Partisans took Kosovo they encountered resistance in several areas, the strongest being in Drenica, where Shaban Polluzha, a former nationalist fighter who had come over to the Partisans, now refused to lead his men north to fight the retreating Germans, arguing that they were needed at home to protect Albanians from attacks by Serbian *Chetnik* or nationalist groups. Martial law was declared in February 1945, and in September Kosovo was formally annexed to Serbia as an "autonomous region," following a request in July by Kosovo's unelected "Regional People's Council" of whose 142 members only 33 were Albanian.[12]

Several points need to be made here to put this in context. The communists of Albania were very much under the tutelage of the Yugoslav party at this stage. This was also a period when many assumed that the Kosovo and the Albanian problem would be solved with the creation of a Balkan Federation, an idea that died with the Soviet-Yugoslav split of 1948. Until then, too, the border with Albania was relatively open. Finally, Tito had concerns about Serbia and the Serbs. Allegedly he told Enver Hoxha in 1946 that "Kosovo and the other Albanian regions belong to you, but not now because the Great Serb reaction would not accept such a thing."[13] To a certain extent, then, Kosovo being part of Serbia, but also a separate region, was a kind of compromise. However there is

Yugoslavia, 1945–1991 (*Map by Peter Winfield*)

also truth in the Serbian claim that it was convenient in terms of the divisions of power within the new state. Serbia was the biggest of the six new Yugoslav republics and the Serbs the most numerous of Yugoslavia's peoples, and the creation of a region for Kosovo and a province for Vojvodina in the north was indeed a way of diluting potential Serbian control, but in an unfair sense in that Serbs in parts of Croatia, say, were not offered the same thing.

The first two decades of communist rule in Kosovo were particularly grim, especially as, in contrast to other parts of Yugoslavia, there was virtually no support for the new regime whatsoever. Kosovo Serbs and Montenegrins, 27.5 percent of the population according to the 1948 census, were suspect because they had shown much more support in Kosovo for the nationalist and royalist *Chetniks* as opposed to their enemies, the Partisans. Albanians, however, were doubly suspect. Few had supported the Partisans and, unlike the Serbs, they did not even want to be part of this state. Thus all of Kosovo's institutions and especially the security services were dominated by Serbs and Montenegrins. Albanian villages were frequently raided for arms, and in 1956 there was an infamous case of several Albanians tried for espionage in Prizren. In 1968 all were released and rehabilitated. From the end of the war until 1966 Yugoslavia's security services were dominated by Aleksandar Ranković, a Serb who was on alert for any whiff of separatism or indeed any other political sin, irrespective of which quarter or nationality it came from.

Several important points: Serbs claim that interwar Serbian settlers were forbidden to return after the war and that, by contrast, large numbers of Albanians from Albania settled in Kosovo before the border was sealed after 1948. They are right up to a point. A decision was initially taken to prevent settlers from returning, but then partially reversed and some did return. An unknown number of Albanians from Albania—"dozens of thousands" says Jean-Arnault Dérens; fewer, say others—almost certainly did come and settle in Kosovo during and especially just after the war, but not the hundreds of thousands claimed by Serbian nationalists.[14]

To a certain extent the arrival of these immigrants was an oddity at this particular moment in time. Indeed, in the context of the time, the Kosovo Albanians are lucky that their fate was only to be reincorporated into Yugoslavia. Quite apart from the flight, expulsion, or resettlement of millions of ethnic Germans, Poles, Ukrainians, and others further north, at the same time as these people were arriving from Albania 350,000 ethnic Germans in Vojvodina and Croatia were being driven out or fleeing, as were many Hungarians from the same areas, as well as Italians from Yugoslav Istria. In the south, Çamëria Albanians, likewise tarred with the brush of collaboration with the Italians and Germans during the war, were also being expelled by the Greeks or in flight. That is not to say that no Albanians left Yugoslavia. Between 1952 and 1967 around 175,000 Muslims emigrated to Turkey. Many of those would have been Macedonian or Bosnian Muslims or ethnic Turks, but the majority are most likely to have been Albanians.

The final important point here is that this was the period when the modern borders of Kosovo were drawn. Preševo/Presheva and Bujanovac/Bujanoc, through which Serbia's main north-south railway ran (and still runs), were excluded, and at this point so was a small part of what is now Serbian-inhabited northern Kosovo, which was added later. The Albanian parts of Macedonia were consigned to that new republic, as were Albanian parts of Montenegro, although the main regions of Albanian settlement there, Ulcinj and Tuzi, are far from Kosovo.

While the fall of Ranković in 1966 is rightly seen as the moment that real change began, both in Kosovo and across Yugoslavia, some changes already predated this. In 1963, for example, Kosovo had been promoted from "region" to "autonomous province" on a par with Vojvodina, although at the same time Kosovo was constitutionally yoked closer to Serbia than to the Yugoslav federation. Slowly but surely, however, an Albanianization of Kosovo also began. Culture began to flourish and in this era of decreased repression Albanians began to be bolder in making demands. In 1968, for example, Kosovo Albanian students, like their counterparts from Prague to Belgrade to Paris, took to the streets. Some shouted, "Long live Enver Hoxha!" More to the point, however, until then Pristina's university had been merely a provincial branch of Belgrade University. The next year it was decided to transform it into a university in its own right. While it was officially bilingual and Serbs did attend, its main role from now on was to be the Albanian-language university for all the Albanians of Yugoslavia.

The other main demand chanted by the students was equally easily dealt with. That was that Kosovo be made a republic, that is, separated from Serbia and given full equality with the existing six Yugoslav republics. This was rejected. Albanians pointed out that there were far more of them than there were, say, Montenegrins or Macedonians, who had their own republics. The reply was that they were "different." The difference was that with the re-creation of Yugoslavia in the wake of the war, its peoples were classed as either "nations" or "nationalities." The nations of Yugoslavia were the Serbs, Croats, Slovenes, Montenegrins, and Macedonians plus, after 1971, the Bosnian Muslims. Nationalities were technically minorities, even if they were more numerous than some nations, because they, like the Kosovo Albanians and Hungarians, were deemed to have motherlands outside of Yugoslavia. Nations had the right to republics, which also had the theoretical right to secede. This was, of course, as good a reason as any for the Albanians never to be given this right, because, not being Slavs and given their history, they might, one day, actually demand to exercise it.

6

FROM THE GOLDEN AGE
TO THE MEMORANDUM

Today the 1970s are seen by Kosovo Albanians as a golden age. They were freer than they had ever been in Yugoslavia and better educated and in better health than they had ever been in the whole of their history. Of course this was not just a golden age for Kosovo, but for Yugoslavia too. Credits poured in from foreign banks, industry developed apace, especially in Slovenia and Croatia, and mass tourism, again especially in Croatia, brought much hard cash. And it was much of this money that built the Kosovo that still exists today, and much of the industry, which does not.

Education was one huge change. Now, for the first time in the 20th century, apart from during the two world wars, children could be educated in Albanian (though they had to learn Serbian too). In 1948, 73 percent of Albanians in Yugoslavia were illiterate.[1] In 1979, 31.5 percent of people in Kosovo were illiterate.[2] That was higher than anywhere else in Yugoslavia, but the majority of those people, Albanians and Serbs, would have been older. In terms of health care, similar huge progress was made. Vaccinations, as elsewhere of course, helped eradicate traditional diseases. This in turn led to a huge increase in population, as, for social and cultural reasons, Albanians continued to have large numbers of children and now far more of them survived. Kosovo Serbs, likewise, had far larger families than Serbs in general, but in terms of demographics this meant that the proportion of Serbs in Kosovo dropped, even if their numbers stayed roughly steady. Serbs were also emigrating, an issue to be examined later.

In terms of culture, a whole new generation of self-confident writers and artists and others began to come of age, and Pristina was increasingly transformed from a sleepy backwater into a modern town. This had advantages and disadvantages. The advantages were that a modern city with modern amenities was being created. The disadvantage was that much of historic old Pristina was destroyed, both literally and in other ways.[3] For example, many old and established Albanian families spoke Turkish among each other, and, similarly, old Serbian families, too, talked Turkish, not to one another, but with their Albanian friends and neighbors. This is a world that has all but vanished, except in Prizren, where remnants of this past linger. Migjen Kelmendi, the writer and newspaper editor, recalls how life began to change in other ways:

> In this period we started to have kind of wealth. There were the first colour televisions and modern furniture and fridges. We started to have a middle class. Everyone was beginning to live like everyone else. The university library started to be built and it felt like we were becoming the real capital of Kosovo. All the streets were being paved with asphalt and asphalt was the symbol of progress. We even called the mayor "Asphalt Nazmi"! At the time they thought they were fighting the old Ottoman heritage and they were building new blocks of flats, and people wanted to live in them. If you lived in an old house it felt very old fashioned.... In 1976, suddenly we had the first

modern cafes. The 1970s were the best period we lived through in this place. After 1981 everything started to decline.[4]

In terms of politics the high point was 1974, when a new Yugoslav constitution redefined Kosovo's place within the country. Kosovo remained a part of Serbia but was almost a full federal entity: It had its own national bank, parliament, government, and police, and thanks to increasing Albanian-ization and the greater numbers of qualified Albanians now able to do the jobs, Albanians were more or less in full control of Kosovo. Apart from its own assembly, its deputies sat in both the Yugoslav federal parliament and the Serbian one.

However, it rankled Albanians that Kosovo still did not have full equality with the republics. Some were arrested and jailed for their opposition to this de facto compromise between Pristina and Belgrade. These hard-line groups were tiny, though, and represented few. At the same time the situation angered Serbs because while Kosovo Albanians sat in the Serbian parliament and thus had a say in the running of Serbia as a whole, the government of Serbia did not have a say in the running of Kosovo. For now, however, Tito was still alive and while he was still alive he was the ultimate arbiter and boss.

Tito died on May 4, 1980. From then on the system he had presided over since 1945 began to unravel, although that this was going to happen with such cataclysmic results was unimaginable at the time. For Kosovo the first major event in this transition from Tito to the destruction of Yugoslavia came less than a year after his death. Its consequences were to be fundamental in shaping the future history of Kosovo. On March 11, 1981, protests started at Pristina University. The spark was not political. The problem was that poor organiza-tion meant that students often had to queue for two hours to get a meal in the canteen. In the days that followed, voices were raised against members of the university administration. Then, members of tiny so-called Marxist-Leninist groups began to get involved. The atmosphere changed. Political demands—above all, that Kosovo should become a republic—began to be raised. Arrests began but these only fueled more protests. Slogans being shouted now included: "We are Albanians, not Yugoslavs!" and "We want a unified Albania!" Schoolchildren and workers now joined in.

The story ended with tanks on the street, special police forces deployed, and a state of emergency. Officially, 57 died in clashes but the real figure could have run into hundreds. Purges of Kosovo's communist party started and a new period of repression set in, albeit one in which, until 1989, Albanians were still in charge. In the eight years following the demonstrations, more than half a million people were at one time either arrested or questioned.

In a very real sense the demonstrations changed the course of history and not just of Kosovo, but also of the whole of Yugoslavia. First, many of the key people who would later set up the Kosovo Liberation Army were imprisoned in or after 1981. This experience was hugely important in radicalizing them against Yugoslavia and Serbia. Second, although Albanians were still in charge in Kosovo, there was a perception that Serbia remained the real power, and thus Serbs were exposed to increased harassment and hostility. This in turn increased their rate of emigration, which thus provided the political platform that Slobodan Milošević could use to his advantage. The unrest in Kosovo also began to alarm other Yugoslavs, a feeling that would, of course, become far more acute later on.

The question of the Kosovo Serbs now began to move to center stage. As noted earlier, Serbs had long been leaving

Kosovo. In the postwar period there was the attraction of jobs in Niš and Belgrade, Kragujevac and Kraljevo. Serbs moved, just as they did from poorer parts of Montenegro and Hercegovina, just as Bosnian Croats gravitated to Croatia. But in Kosovo, apart from these "pull" factors, there was also the "push" factor. Initially, after the war, Serbs had dominated the province, not just in terms of power and jobs. With the changing political climate, better education for Albanians, and the Albanianization of the province, Serbs lost their privileged status.

Demography played its role, too. As noted, census statistics are not that reliable, but they do provide a good guide to trends. For example, in 1948, there were 199,961 Serbs and Montenegrins in Kosovo, or 27.5 percent of the population. At the same time there were 498,242 Albanians or 68.5 percent of the population. After that the numbers of Serbs and Montenegrins climbed a little, to peak in 1964 at 264,604 or 20.9 percent. But, by now, the Albanian population had grown to 646,805 or 67.2 percent. By 1981 the Serbian and Montenegrin figure had dropped to 236,526, while the Albanian population had soared to more than 1.2 million, or an Albanian percentage of 77.4 as against 14.9 percent Serbs and Montenegrins. In 1991 the Albanian figure was more than 1.6 million, or 82.2 percent, as against 215,346 Serbs and Montenegrins, who then made up 10.9 percent of Kosovo's people.[5]

In other words emigration meant that while the Serbian and Montenegrin population stayed relatively steady, in terms of numbers, their proportion as a percentage of the population shrank in the face of the Albanian population explosion. This was to lead to a veritable land hunger. So some Serbs felt they were harassed to leave their farms and houses, while at the same time the large amount of money being offered for them meant that they could get far more for their money in Serbia proper. So we can see that it is hard to say which was predominant—the pull or the push factors. In general terms it is probably safe to say that both were present, and that, after 1981, the scales, for many, may have tipped somewhat.

Branislav Krstić, a Serbian journalist who now lives in North Mitrovica, grew up in Djakovica/Gjakova. He was born in 1964 and his family fled from their hometown in 1999. His story provides valuable insight into growing up in the late 1970s and his own experience of 1981. Both of his parents were Kosovo Serbs. His mother used to warn him to "be careful of Albanians." In the 1970s, he recalls, "Serbs were only 10 percent of the population of Djakovica, but they used to be much more."

> I remember when my best friends moved to Belgrade. Almost every year, families from my neighborhood moved there. When I was growing up my street was 90 percent Serbian and even officially called Serbian Street (*Srpska Ulica*)... Bearing in mind what my mother told me, I was still friends with Albanians and that helped me learn Albanian well....Albanian friends used to visit me at home and I was invited to theirs too, but this was unusual. Typically people were quite friendly but generally they did not go to each other's homes.

Things began to change immediately as the demonstrations began in Kosovo in 1981. Krstić was 16 years old and, at first, the television news did not report what was happening and they were told not to come to school. Krstić made the mistake of asking his Albanian teacher why the student protests had not been on television when "we could see what was happening in Lebanon or other places where there was conflict."

He told me to wait five minutes. The he came back with the head and then I was taken to see the director of all the schools in Djakovica, an Albanian. He was very aggressive. He asked me if I wanted to see how the police were beating Albanian kids and said that I was a Serbian nationalist and that he would do all he could to see that my father lost his job and that it would be best if my family left Djakovica.

Krstić's conclusion? In 1981 the atmosphere changed, he says, but "the largest slice of power was in the hands of the Albanians. When Slobodan Milošević came to power...every- ✓ thing remained the same, only the power was transferred into the hands of Serbs."[6]

Foreigners remember that the Yugoslav wars began in Slovenia (or maybe they have forgotten that one), then moved to Croatia and Bosnia, and only then to Kosovo, with small follow-on conflicts in south Serbia and Macedonia. Former Yugoslavs of course remember it somewhat differently: that the conflict that destroyed the country began in Kosovo. The key date is 1989, when Serbia, under Slobodan Milošević, abolished its autonomy. But what was the buildup to it, especially in the wake of the 1981 riots? The takeover did not come out of the blue.

As early as 1969 the Serbian Orthodox Church had begun to compile figures about the gradual exodus of Serbs from Kosovo. Dobrica Ćosić, a former Partisan commander and then a novelist and later Yugoslav president under Milošević, had in 1968 been expelled from the Communist Party for, among other things, declaring that Kosovo's Albanian leaders were separatists. However, it was only after Tito's death that people began to lose their fear of the communist state, and petitions began to be circulated concerning the fate of the Kosovo Serbs.

In 1984, Ćosić suggested that the venerable Serbian Academy of Sciences and Arts address various issues concerning the future of the Serbs as a whole. Sixteen intellectuals, not including him, began that process. Then, in September 1986, a Serbian newspaper leaked extracts of the draft. What was published was explosive. It was a key moment in the story of the destruction of Yugoslavia.

Most of the so-called Memorandum is dull, worthy, and addresses perfectly legitimate concerns, including the economy, in ordinary language. It raised the issue that 24 percent of Serbs lived outside Serbia (mostly in Bosnia and Croatia), but that number went up to 40.3 percent if you included Kosovo and Vojvodina. Then, however, the language suddenly became shrill, indeed quite hysterical, asserting that the Kosovo Serbs were being subjected to "genocide." In one of its most infamous paragraphs it states that "the physical, political, legal, and cultural genocide of the Serbian population of Kosovo and Metohija is a worse historical defeat than any experienced in the liberation wars waged by Serbia from the First Serbian Uprising in 1804 to the uprising of 1941." Serbs were faced with a reign of terror, it stated, and that

> unless things change radically, in less than ten years' time there will no longer be any Serbs left in Kosovo, and "ethnically pure" Kosovo, that unambiguously stated goal of the Greater Albanian racists...will be achieved....Kosovo's fate remains a vital question for the entire Serbian nation. If it is not resolved...if genuine security and unambiguous equality for all peoples living in Kosovo and Metohija are not established; if objective and permanent conditions for the return of the expelled nation are not created, then this part of the Republic

of Serbia and Yugoslavia will become a European issue, with the gravest possible unforeseeable consequences.

According to the Memorandum, Serbia's leaders were guilty for letting things have got this bad, just as they were for a similar situation, which they described in Croatia. What should be done? "Serbia must not be passive and wait and see what others will say, as it has done in the past."[7] The significance of the Memorandum in laying the intellectual foundations of what was to follow, first in Kosovo and then across the rest of Yugoslavia, cannot be underestimated.

7

THE MILOŠEVIĆ-RUGOVA YEARS

Slobodan Milošević was the right man (or the wrong one, of course) in the right place at the right time. He was born in 1941 to Montenegrin parents in Požarevac, close to Belgrade. When Milošević was small his father left the family and then, in 1962, committed suicide. In 1972 his communist-activist mother killed herself, too. At school he gained the reputation of being a serious student. There he met Mira Marković, who came from an important communist family. She was the love of his life and, many believe, the driving force behind him.

At university the couple met Ivan Stambolić, a man who also had an important Communist Party family background. A fast friend, Stambolić rose through the party ranks and took Milošević with him. By 1984 Stambolić was head of the Serbian Communist Party and Milošević head of the Belgrade party. In 1986 Stambolić moved up a notch. He became president of Serbia, so Milošević inherited his position as head of the Serbian party.

In April 1987 Stambolić sent Milošević to listen to the complaints of Kosovo Serbs in Kosovo Polje/Fushë Kosova, just outside Pristina. Stambolić had for some time been complaining about the problem of Kosovo voting against

Serbia in the rotating federal presidency, which had succeeded
Tito, and of Kosovo having a say in Serbia's affairs while Serbia
had no say in Kosovo's. When Milošević got to Kosovo Polje,
the Serbs were clashing with police, throwing stones at them.
Milošević emerged from the building where the meeting was
taking place and then uttered the words that would immor-
talize him: "No one should dare to beat you." He returned
to the building to listen to the grievances of ordinary Serbs
and made a rousing speech demanding that they stand up to
oppression and promising shame if the Serbs were to leave
Kosovo. In terms of a communist state, and of Yugoslavia, this
was electric. It was also staged. Four days before, Milošević
had already been in Kosovo to set up the whole event.

Milošević, who until then had been a rather anonymous,
gray, apparatchik, had read the situation in the country and the
world well. Communism was dying, although this was far from
apparent to the vast majority of people. Milošević knew that
by playing the nationalist card he could secure both supreme
power in Serbia, and then hopefully Yugoslavia, and also
survive the demise of communism. Some of this was to come
true. By playing on the issue of the plight of the Kosovo Serbs
Milošević did indeed become extraordinarily popular among
the Serbs. His intention was then to dominate Yugoslavia.
This was where he miscalculated. He destroyed it instead. The
actions he was to take over the next few years propelled him to
extraordinary power and popularity, but by stripping Kosovo
of its autonomy and using tanks to do so, he instilled fear elsewhere, which in turn fueled the rise of nationalism in other
parts of the country. In that sense, those who argue that the end
of Yugoslavia began in Kosovo are right.

Several key events need to be noted now. On September 3,
1987, a young Kosovo Albanian conscript killed four others—a

Serb, two Bosnians, and a Slovene—in the town of Paračin, in Serbia, where they were based, before killing himself.[1] Instead of reporting that this was the act of someone who had gone mad, the Serbian press reported that the soldier had been part of a nationalist plot. Ten thousand people then turned out at the funeral of the young Serb. Three weeks later, and in part riding on the anti-Albanian mood that had been fueled by the Paračin murders, Miloševic turned on his former mentor at the Eighth Session of the Central Committee of the Serbian communists. It was a key moment. Stunned, Stambolić was destroyed by the man he had counted as his friend. He resigned as president three months later.

Over the next two years Milošević moved to consolidate his power, by convening so-called Meetings of Truth in which millions were eventually to hear and to feel a Serbia rising from what would soon be the ashes of Yugoslavia. "Who betrays Kosovo, betrays the people," chanted the crowds. Serbs were being oppressed in Kosovo, they were told; Serbia was being exploited by Slovenia and Croatia, and Serbia's leaders were out of touch with what the people demanded. By October 1988 Milošević had secured the fall of the government of Vojvodina, and Montenegro was to follow in January 1989. Kosovo was to prove an altogether harder nut to crack.

In November 1989, Milošević told a rally of hundreds of thousands in Ušće, in Belgrade, "Every nation has a love which eternally warms its heart. For Serbia it is Kosovo. That is why Kosovo will remain in Serbia."[2] He had just succeeded in having Kosovo's two main leaders, Azem Vlassi and Kaqusha Jashari, removed and Albanian miners from Trepča/Trepça were protesting against this. But Milošević's pressure was relentless. In January Milošević succeeded in installing his own "loyal Albanians," as they were called.

The next month, as preparations were being made to abolish the essence of Kosovo's autonomy, the Trepça miners began protesting again, this time with a hunger strike. Others began to protest as well. It was to no avail. On March 23, 1989, Kosovo's assembly building was surrounded by police and tanks, and deputies voted in favor of constitutional amendments that would restore Serbia's power over the province. Kosovo as a province however, was not abolished. Milošević needed its vote on the federal presidency, which had eight members. With Serbia, Montenegro, Vojvodina, and now Kosovo in the bag, Milošević needed just one more and he would be the master of Yugoslavia. He would never get this vote. Yugoslavia was disintegrating, and Milošević's actions had fueled the rise of nationalism elsewhere, particularly in Croatia. The Slovenes, too, had had enough. They were heading for the exit, but in the run up to the end the Slovene leadership made clear their sympathy with the Kosovo Albanians and the Trepça miners in particular.

The end of Kosovo's autonomy was greeted with violent protests by Albanians, but eventually they were crushed. During the unrest thousands of police poured in from outside the province, and widespread repression, arrests, and imprisonments followed, coupled with hundreds of new laws and regulations that needed to be passed to integrate Kosovo back into Serbia. On June 28, 1989, the 600th anniversary of the Battle of Kosovo, Milošević celebrated his victory at Gazimestan, which is the part of the battlefield, where a tower commemorates it. There, hundreds of thousands of Serbs gathered—by some estimates there were a million people—plus the Serbian Orthodox Patriarch and, feeling very uneasy, the rest of Yugoslavia's leaders. Milošević invoked the spirit of the Serbs who had died in battle and during the world wars, and then uttered the famous, prophetic phrase that is now engraved on the history of the people of all of the former Yugoslavia: "Six centuries later, again we are in battles and quarrels. They are not armed battles, though such things should not be excluded yet."[3]

The destruction of Yugoslavia and its collapse in blood is a story that has been widely told elsewhere. On June 25, 1991, Slovenia and Croatia declared their independence. In the former, this was followed by a ten-day war and then the withdrawal of the Yugoslav army. They were needed elsewhere to help draw the borders around the Greater Serbia, encompassing Serbian regions of Croatia and Bosnia that Milošević now intended to create.

The war in Croatia was appalling. It included the siege of Vukovar, in which the town was virtually leveled, and the siege of the historic port of Dubrovnik.

In 1992 Bosnia collapsed in war, too. Sarajevo, its capital, was besieged by Serbian forces until the end in 1995. Some 100,000 died including, most notoriously of all, more than 7,000 Bosniak men and boys, killed after the fall of the eastern Bosnian town of Srebrenica. This was a seminal event and its importance in changing the course of history in Kosovo is not widely understood. The fact that this massacre had happened in a zone that the UN Security Council had pledged to protect was seared into the consciences of Western leaders and goes a long way to explaining why, in 1999, they were prepared to move fast to bomb Serbia because of Kosovo, fearful that such a thing would happen again. This is to get ahead of our story, though.

The collapse of Yugoslavia and the bloody events elsewhere simply eclipsed Kosovo. For years, little news filtered out of the province, not because it was not accessible, but because what happened here simply could not compete in terms of news with what was happening elsewhere. However, several important dates and moves need to be noted. The first is December 23, 1989, which saw the foundation of the Democratic League of Kosovo (LDK) with Ibrahim Rugova at its head. The party, which was really a broad-based political movement, quickly absorbed former Communist Party members and was to become the main focus of opposition to Serbian rule from then until the Kosovo war in 1998. The use of the word "league" in its name was of course designed to recall the League of Prizren of 1878.

On July 2, 1990, 114 out of 123 Albanian members of Kosovo's parliament, which had earlier and under duress voted to extinguish Kosovo's autonomy, now cast their ballots to establish Kosovo as a republic on equal terms with the six other Yugoslav republics. The Serbian parliament voted to annul this act. On September 7 the Kosovar deputies, meeting secretly in Kačanik/Kaçanik, voted for a constitution for their republic. At this point independence was not on the agenda because, although the war had started, Yugoslavia still existed. It was only on September 21, 1991, that they declared independence, a move confirmed first by a referendum, deemed illegal by the Serbian authorities of course, and finally confirmed in parliament on October 19, 1991.

Now a virtual state, the Republic of Kosova came into being, existing in a weird, parallel form to the Serbian authorities, who were very much in charge. Indeed, Serbian authority under Milošević, and after the breakout of the Bosnian war, was to stretch from Kosovo to the borders of Hungary, to encompass some one-third of Croatian territory and 70 percent of Bosnia-Hercegovina. In Croatia, a Republic of Serbian Krajina was created, which covered that territory taken by the Serbs and where Serbs lived. In Bosnia, the Republika Srpska was founded, which, unlike its Croatian counterpart, survived the war and is now one of the two entities that make up the state.

On May 24, 1992, Kosovo Albanians held an election for president and parliament. These were strange elections because, while illegal in the eyes of the Serbs and held in private houses instead of public buildings, the Serbs did little or nothing to impede them. There was good reason for this. The first was that Ibrahim Rugova and the LDK had embraced a philosophy of nonviolence. The second was that, simultaneous to these events, the siege of Sarajevo was beginning. Milošević had no reason to provoke conflict in Kosovo. Indeed the Croats, under their president Franjo Tudjman, had sent feelers to the Albanians, asking them to open a second front against the Serbs, a request that was brusquely rejected by the Kosovars who thought this would mean that they would simply become cannon fodder for the Croats. The Croats, who have as long a memory as anyone else, have not forgotten this rebuff. The Albanians, however, unlike the Croats, had no way to arm themselves. Meanwhile, the fact that the LDK decreed that Kosovo Albanians should have nothing to do with the Serbian state meant quite simply that Slobodan Milošević could stay in power. If they had voted in Serbian elections, Milošević could not have remained president, because his margin of victory from 1992 onward in all Serbian elections would never have been enough. This suited the Kosovo Albanians, though. They were horrified by the ethnic cleansing and wars that were taking place in Croatia and Bosnia and, not having the means to defend themselves, felt Rugova's strategy was the right one for the times. Besides, if the policy of the Serbs was, as the slogan went, "all Serbs in one state," then why should they object? If that was good for Serbs then the world would find it hard to object if they demanded that all Albanians should live in one state, too.

However, as Rugova and the LDK busied themselves creating parallel institutions to run the lives of Kosovo's Albanians, and complained of human rights abuses at the hands of the Serbs, Rugova also garnered credit for what was perceived as his righteous policy of peaceful resistance. Thus he was often called the "Gandhi of the Balkans." This was a total misunderstanding, but for the Kosovo Albanians, a happy one. The policy was based on the hard fact that war, at this stage, would simply mean that the Albanians would lose and risk being ethnically cleansed. In 1992, Rugova said, "We are not certain how strong the Serbian military presence in the province actually is, but we do know that it is over-whelming and that we have nothing to set against the tanks and other modern weaponry in Serbian hands." He then added, "We would have no chance of successfully resisting the army. In fact the Serbs only wait for a pretext to attack the Albanian population and wipe it out. We believe it is better to do nothing and stay alive than to be massacred."[4]

Of course Milošević was happy that the Albanians should adopt this strategy and, fighting in Croatia and Bosnia, he had no reason to want to fight in Kosovo as well. However, it is worth remembering something that seems to have been forgotten as a mere footnote to history. That is that on December 24, 1992, the first President George Bush sent a note to Milošević, which became known as the "Christmas warning." Bush was leaving the presidency within weeks, but the note was unambiguous. It said: "In the event of conflict in Kosovo caused by Serbian actions, the U.S. will be prepared to employ military force against Serbians in Kosovo and Serbia proper."[5]

Ibrahim Rugova was an unusual figure. He was born in 1944. Six weeks later, as the communist Partisans restored Yugoslav control over Kosovo, they executed his father and

grandfather. In 1976 he spent a year in Paris studying under
Roland Barthes. He returned to Kosovo to become a professor
of Albanian literature. From then on he cultivated a bohe-
mian air. He always wore a silk scarf, except in August. He
was partial to drink and a heavy smoker, which may well
explain his death from lung cancer in 2006. Rugova became
head of the LDK almost by accident. When it was formed in
1989 he was dispatched to ask Rexhep Qosja, the prominent
nationalist writer, to lead it. Qosja refused, and to prevent
someone else nobody much liked from becoming leader the
party's founders gave the job to Rugova, at that time regarded
as something of an outsider even though he was head of the
Writers' Union. After that, and especially after he was elected
president of Kosovo in 1992, Rugova's life settled down into a
very strange pattern. His office was a small wooden bungalow
close to Pristina's football stadium. He was driven there in
a black presidential-style Audi, and his office issued daily
communiqués about whom the president of the republic had
seen and what he had done. Ordinary people came to pay
court and ask favors of the man they increasingly came to
regard as the father of the nation. Oddly for a national figure,
he was extraordinarily boring to talk to or to interview, and his
lack of charisma made his popularity all the more unusual.

While Serbia kept the province under a tight clamp,
frequently making raids for arms and arresting anyone they
suspected of subversion—some of which was real—Fehmi
Agani, the real brains behind Rugova's operation (he was
killed by Serbian police in 1999) and others plotted to make
the phantom republic they had declared real. Its most visible
component was education. In the wake of Serbia's reintegra-
tion of the province, the vast majority of Albanians in any
form of public service jobs were sacked or in effect forced

out. If they were not sacked, they were asked to sign loyalty oaths, which if they had, would have meant being branded a traitor by other Albanians. In schools, teachers were told that they would now be teaching the Serbian curriculum, not the former Kosovo one, which they refused to do, leading to the dismissal, by March 1991, of 21,000 teachers. Similarly, 1,855 doctors and other medical staff were sacked.[6]

Rugova's shadow government now set about reemploying as many of these people as possible. But to do that, he had to be able to pay them. All Kosovo Albanians were now asked to pay 3 percent income tax and companies a 10 percent profit tax into the coffers of his shadow government, and networks of people were organized to collect the money. Even more valuable perhaps than the contributions made at home, however, were those made by the diaspora. Collecting money from them was organized by Bujar Bukoshi, a former surgeon who left Kosovo after "independence" on October 19, 1991, in order to set up a government-in-exile of which he was premier and foreign minister. After some false starts it eventually ended up near Bonn. The tax-raising system worked well because first, most Kosovo Albanians felt the need for solidarity at this point (in contrast to the postwar period) and second, anyone who did not contribute could be ostracized.

The education received in the parallel system was rudimentary but it was a system that worked. It also meant that for the first time since 1918 Serbia had no say whatsoever in the content of what pupils were taught. This meant that now, like their Serbian counterparts, young Kosovo Albanians grew up immersed in a nationalist culture quite divorced from the "Brotherhood and Unity" of the Yugoslav days. Serbs and Albanians now learned quite different histories of Kosovo and the region, and Albanians no longer learned Serbian either.

The system was vast. In primary education in 1998 there were 266,413 pupils; in secondary schools there were 58,700; and then there were 16,000 in the parallel university.[7]

Health care was organized by a humanitarian organization named for Mother Teresa. It employed hundreds of doctors and nurses, and also supplied food where necessary. Some doctors did, however, stay in hospitals because of the equipment, and, when necessary, Albanians did go to hospital either in Kosovo or Serbia proper.

During this period large (but unknown) numbers of Kosovo Albanians went abroad, mainly because there were so few opportunities to work in Kosovo, where Serbs were now in full control and all significant jobs in the administration and public service were taken by them. Serbs often grumbled though, especially as hyperinflation caught hold of wartime Serbia and their wages were reduced to nothing. The reason was that many Albanians, having been turfed out of their state jobs, had had to set up small businesses and so were often not as badly off as their state-employed Serbian neighbors. Serbs and Albanians led increasingly parallel lives. Rona Nishliu, who was born in Mitrovica in 1986, sums up something of the atmosphere of those years:

> When I went to school, we Albanians went in the afternoon and Serbs went in the morning. We did not have any contacts with them and we could not use the gym or the laboratories. They were locked, so we did sport outside. We did have Serbian neighbors. People we said "hello" or "good afternoon" to, but I did not have any Serbian friends. Both my parents used to work for the Trepça mining complex but both were kicked out in 1989. After that my father ran a shop and my mother was at home.[8]

8
THE WAR

The second part of the Kosovo war, the 78-day bombardment of Serbia, including Kosovo and also Montenegro, in 1999, was so spectacular that it is easy for foreigners to forget the prologue to this tragic drama: the preceding year of conflict between the Kosovo Liberation Army (KLA), the Ushtria Çlirimtare e Kosovës (UCK), and Serbian forces. Moreover, in the sequence of events that led to war, two of the most significant had absolutely nothing to do with Kosovo at all. Kosovo is an integral part of the region it is situated in: just as many of the roots of the Yugoslav conflict lay in Kosovo, likewise, events in Bosnia and Albania were now to change the course of Kosovo's history.

The KLA has to rank as one of the most successful military organizations in history. Its success has nothing to do with its military prowess; it won no battles. It is, rather, thanks to the fact that emerging on to the scene at the right place, at the right time, it was able to have NATO win its war for it.

The KLA's origins were, until it appeared, shrouded in mystery and intrigue and, as is the nature of such things, its ancestry lay in a network of tiny overlapping and feuding so-called Marxist-Leninist groups. Since the end of the Second

World War the authorities in Kosovo had occasionally unearthed small, subversive groups dedicated to detaching Kosovo from Serbia and Yugoslavia. One, for example, was founded by Adem Demaçi, a man who, between 1958 and his final release in 1990, was to spend a combined total of 28 years in prison. He was to become known as the Nelson Mandela of the Balkans and served as an inspiration for generations of young Kosovo Albanian nationalists who followed in his wake.

Without a doubt, however, the most significant events to galvanize the tiny, hard-line nationalist groups of Kosovo were the demonstrations of 1981. To a certain extent, the fact that these protests, which began about conditions at the university, were rapidly channeled into a political direction is testament to the fact that, small as they were, these groups were more influential than their numbers might suggest. However, even more important, in terms of the founding of the KLA, was that many of those who were to play key roles in that story were profoundly affected by the events of 1981 and its aftermath.

A note of clarification: The tiny groups that were to serve as the forerunners of the KLA and its political wing, the Popular Movement for Kosova or the Lëvizja Popullore e Kosovës (LPK), were often called Marxist-Leninist or Enverist, after Albania's communist dictator, Enver Hoxha. This is misleading. Although initially, at least, their ideas were expressed in Marxist jargon, they were not Marxists, or even Enverists. Instead, they were old-fashioned nationalists. In this period, the problem was that Yugoslavia enjoyed huge prestige around the world. Calling for its destruction and the creation of a Greater Albania was hardly the way to win friends and influence people, nor for that matter an idea that sounded anything other than simply crazy. Thus Enverism and Marxism were, to a great extent, a mask and a way to avoid being tarred with the brush of Fascism, too, as Albanian nationalism could, at that time, be easily condemned as nothing more than the resurgence of wartime nationalist and collaborationist ideas. Conversely, an added advantage to identifying with the Albanian regime was that these groups could, in return, expect some modest help, financial and otherwise.

The KLA was founded in December 1993. However, one of the key events leading to this took place in a village near Stuttgart in Germany on January 17, 1982, when three Kosovar activists, Kadri Zeka and the brothers Jusuf and Bardhosh Gërvalla, were assassinated. They had been meeting to discuss the union of their two respective Marxist groups. Most Albanians have always assumed that they were killed by the Yugoslav secret services, although another theory holds that they were killed by Albania's intelligence services. Jusuf Gërvalla especially had been popular and well known as a journalist in Pristina. The death of these three was taken as a declaration of war by some of the men who were close to them or moved in the same circles. At home they distributed leaflets and held clandestine meetings, and in the diaspora they worked hard to disseminate their political ideas and some even began military training.

Over the next decade or more they also began to attract a new generation of activists, many of whom moved back and forth between Kosovo and the diaspora communities of Switzerland and elsewhere. Two of the most notable were Hashim Thaçi, later the wartime political head of the KLA and the prime minister of Kosovo when it declared independence, and Ramush Haradinaj, who became one of the most important wartime leaders of the KLA in western Kosovo, and then, for some three months, prime minister, before resigning in 2005 to answer charges of war crimes at the UN's Yugoslav war crimes tribunal in The Hague.[1]

During the 1980s, occasional bombs could be put down to various tiny subversive groups in Kosovo. The number of these began to mount gradually during the 1990s, including the odd murder of Serbian officials and people considered to be collaborators of the Serbs. At the same time, discussions were held with Bujar Bukoshi, Rugova's prime minister in exile. In 1990, some members of the group, which was to later to be known as the LPK, received some training in an Albanian military base. One of them was Adem Jashari, a kind of modern-day *kaçak* whose death, after his house was besieged by the Serbs in Prekaz in 1998, was to provide the KLA and Kosovo, as we saw earlier, with a martyr. In 1991 and 1992 another group trained in Albania, but this time they did so alongside Kosovo Albanian policemen and officers of the Yugoslav army, who were loyal to Bukoshi. On their return many were arrested and killed.

From then on the cooperation between the LPK cum KLA and Rugova's people was difficult and frequently deeply antagonistic. The LPK regarded Rugova as a kind of Serbian collaborator. In turn, most LDK people regarded the LPK as activists on the extreme fringe of politics who risked bringing down disaster upon their people. It was not that Rugova and others were against war as such, but, rather, as we have noted, that since there was no means for the Kosovo Albanians to arm themselves properly there was no credible way to wage it. The problem, retorted the LPK and the people connected with them, was that this policy was not actually resulting in much either, a claim that became harder to resist after the end of wars in Bosnia and Croatia.

Although the KLA was founded in 1993, it was only in 1996 that most members of even the LPK began to hear about what was happening. The next year this tiny band—then perhaps just 150 men—began to take action, attacking Serbian policemen and people they regarded as Albanian collaborators. On January 31, 1997, the KLA took its first casualties. Three died, including Zahir Pajaziti, the "Chief of the Supreme Command of the KLA." Today he is commemorated in the statue that stands opposite the Hotel Grand in Pristina. At the time he died, Rugova was keen to dismiss stories of possible rivals to his power and influence and when asked about the gradually increasing numbers of attacks in Kosovo, he claimed that these were the work of the Serbian secret police.

Politically and strategically, two key events were to change everything in Kosovo. The first was the November 1995 Dayton peace agreement, which ended the Bosnian war. In the wake of this, most international sanctions against what was then the Federal Republic of Yugoslavia, that is, Serbia and Montenegro, were lifted, and the European Union recognized this state, which had been born in 1992, as the successor to the old Yugoslavia of six republics. This was a huge trauma for Kosovo's Albanians. Dayton was about Bosnia yet it also marked the effective end of hostilities between Serbia and Croatia, too.

Kosovo was not an issue at Dayton, but for the LPK it was a moment to savor as it meant that they could argue that they had always been right that peaceful resistance would get their people nowhere. From that moment on, the tide began to turn in their favor. But that was far from enough. Talking about armed resistance was one thing, as was the odd killing of a Serbian policeman or hapless Kosovo Albanian employed by Serbia's forestry service and thus regarded as a collaborator, but a full-scale uprising against the Serbs? How could this happen with no access to arms? "We continuously had huge problems with the lack of weapons," Ramush Haradinaj recalled later. "This was the reason why many of our planned operations were not carried out."[2]

In the spring of 1997, the most unexpected thing happened: Albania collapsed into complete anarchy. This happened when financial pyramid, or "Ponzi," schemes that the government had tolerated came to their natural, crashing end. In the chaos that followed, the government of President Sali Berisha lost control, the opposition Socialists mobilized their supporters, especially in the south, to rise up against him, and in the ensuing mayhem armories across Albania were simply abandoned by the military and security forces and looted. Suddenly, hundreds of thousands of weapons were available, including and above all, Kalashnikov rifles, for as little as $5 each. It was, as Haradinaj said in something of an understatement, a situation "which created good conditions for us in terms of supplies."[3] The risks remained high, though. On an arms run in May 1997, for example, Haradinaj's brother Luan was killed.

Though the strategic situation was changing, this was not immediately obvious to everyone; however, several key events began to make it so. On October 1, 1997, a demonstration of 20,000 students in Pristina led to clashes with the police. Among their leaders was Albin Kurti, who would later lead the Vetëvendosje, or Self Determination, movement that would oppose the UN in Kosovo after the war. The students had been in touch with the LPK, which was sending them money. On October 15 Adrian Krasniqi became the first KLA man to die in uniform. When his funeral was held a few days later, 13,000 people turned up. Then on November 28, the Albanian national day, some 20,000 came to the funeral of a teacher and political activist killed accidentally when the KLA had attacked a Serbian police patrol. Three KLA men turned up and announced in public, "Serbia is massacring Albanians. The KLA is the only force which is fighting for the liberation and national unity of Kosovo!"

On January 22, 1998, the police tried to arrest Adem Jashari, but they were repulsed. One month later, as tensions continued to mount, Robert Gelbard, the U.S. special envoy to the region, criticized Serbian police violence but also described the KLA as a terrorist group. Perhaps Slobodan Milošević interpreted this as an invitation to act. Certainly Rugova did not know what to do. He kept quiet. Fighting began in the village of Likošane/Likoshan on February 28. It was to culminate a few days later when Serbian security forces, after a three-day siege, finally took Adem Jashari's family compound in Prekaz. He was killed, along with 20 members of his extended family and others, including women and children, making a total of 51 dead. There was now no going back. Jashari's image, replete with bushy beard and white, domed Albanian *plis* felt hat, would become ubiquitous and the man himself elevated to the status of virtual saint.

The Serbian police started to dig fortifications. Kosovo Albanians were overtaken by a mix of conflicting emotions. Fear was one of them, but another, euphoria, was stronger, especially as the KLA began to take territory in the central Drenica region and in the west. More and more young men began to trek over the mountains to Albania to collect weapons, and in the diaspora more and more people began to give to the KLA's Homeland Calling fund instead of contributing to Rugova's coffers.

The KLA itself was unprepared for what was now happening, not least because it did not fully control the situation on the ground—many villages arming themselves and, with little link to the KLA, calling themselves KLA. Most significantly, during this period, the KLA was establishing itself in areas that were almost entirely ethnic Albanian and, for now, Serbian forces were making no real concerted effort to fight back. Serbian civilians and many other non-Albanians from these areas fled or were ethnically cleansed. Some were murdered. Various diplomatic missions came and went, attempting to seek a peace deal. The only man who would count now was Richard Holbrooke, the tough American diplomat who had overseen the Dayton deal. He had been invited to see what he could do by Rugova. Gelbard had, by calling the KLA terrorists, made enemies among the Albanians and Milošević, too, had taken up against him. But Milošević respected Holbrooke. His mission began in earnest in May 1997.

A few weeks later, the situation on the ground began to turn. Overconfident, a KLA commander decided to seize an important coal mine. It was held for barely six days. The next month a unit attacked the Trepča mine and then the town of Orahovac/Rahovec, which had a mixed Albanian and Serbian population. Four days later, utterly devastated, it was back in Serbian hands. The counteroffensive now began in earnest. The Serbian police, backed up by the army, began to slice through KLA areas. Villages began to burn and tens of thousands fled. By August 3 the UN's refugee agency, the UNHCR, estimated that 200,000 Kosovars had been displaced. The KLA was proving it was no match for Serbian forces when they began to fight back. But Milošević's Serbian authorities were also proving how inept they were in terms of the war for international public opinion. As in Croatia and Bosnia, they were simply herding large numbers of terrified people straight into the arms of the foreign media.

In view of what subsequently happened, it is interesting to note what Madeleine Albright, then the U.S. secretary of state, thought, as recorded in her memoirs. Talking about the KLA, she writes, "My own view of the fighters was mixed. I sympathized with their opposition to Milošević, understood their desire for independence, and accepted that force was sometimes necessary for a just cause to prevail." But, she went on,

> on the other hand, there did not appear to be much Jeffersonian thinking within the KLA. Often indiscriminate in their attacks, they seemed intent on provoking a massive Serb response so that international intervention would be unavoidable. I wanted to stop Milošević from marauding through Kosovo, but I didn't want that determination exploited by the KLA for purposes we opposed. We therefore took pains to insist that we would not operate as the KLA's air force or rescue the KLA if it got into trouble as a result of its own actions. We condemned violence by either side.[4]

The diplomats tried a number of tacks. They talked to both sides, they initiated meetings between Serbs and Albanians, and they also instituted patrols by diplomats on the ground to report back what was happening. This, the Kosovo Diplomatic Observer Mission (KDOM), which was created by Holbrooke, was later superseded by the Kosovo Verification Mission (KVM), which was supposed to constitute some 2,000 monitors under the auspices of the Organization for Security and Cooperation in Europe (OSCE), with help from NATO in the air, to verify an agreement made between Milošević and Holbrooke to reduce Serbian forces to their prewar level. Holbrooke managed to extract the agreement because behind him he had a credible threat of the use of force by NATO.

The KLA, however, was not party to the agreement and it soon began to unravel. The KLA had been virtually defeated in the summer fighting. Now it had an opportunity to rearm and reorganize. The agreement was, recalled Haradinaj, "life saving."[5] One reason was that, as he explains it, ordinary people had lost faith in the KLA but visits by important foreigners to its commanders on the ground helped restore its credibility.

Toward the end of the year it was clear that the deal with Serbia could not hold. The number of clashes began multiplying, as did ugly incidents of pure terror, such as the gunning down of six Serbian teenagers in the Panda Café in Peć/Peja on December 14. On January 8 the KLA killed three Serbian policemen near the town of Štimlje/Shtime. Two days later, another was killed. The Serbs prepared an offensive against the KLA-held village of Račak/Reçak. When they had finished 45 people, including a 12-year-old boy and a woman, were found dead by a trench. It appeared that they had been executed after the Serbs took the village, and William Walker, the American head of the KVM, accused them of this. They refuted it, saying that they were fighters whose bodies had been moved by the KLA after the battle to make it look like a massacre.

In the wake of Račak, the diplomats decided on one last push to make a deal. Serbs and Albanians were called to meet in a chateau southeast of Paris, in the town of Rambouillet. They were asked to look at proposals for Kosovo's future, which had been worked out by Chris Hill, an American diplomat, and Wolfgang Petritsch, an Austrian. Russia also sent a negotiator. The Albanian delegation included the most important Kosovo

Albanian personalities, such as Rugova, Bukoshi, Agani, and, from the KLA side, Thaçi and Xhavit Haliti, one of the KLA's founding fathers. Thaçi was selected by a vote to head the delegation, which also included Veton Surroi, a journalist and politician who had long been active on many fronts in favor of Kosovo and who was also the founder of the leading daily paper *Koha Ditore*. The Serbian team was essentially made up of nonentities, picked because they were Kosovo Turks, Roma, Muslims, and others. The only man who counted on the Serbian side was Milošević, and he was in Belgrade.

The "talks," such as they were, opened on February 6 and lasted until February 23. In essence, the deal presented to the parties and finessed in Rambouillet proposed several things. The first was that the agreement would have a limited duration of three years. Some Serbian and Yugoslav forces could stay in Kosovo, especially on the borders. Kosovo would be an autonomous part of Serbia and security would be guaranteed by a NATO-led force, and the KLA would have to disarm.

Milošević, counting perhaps on Russian support and divisions within NATO, rejected the plan. He did not want NATO troops in Kosovo and objected to a provision (which he never tried to negotiate away and which he might well have succeeded in doing had he wanted to) by which NATO troops would be able to move through the rest of Yugoslavia. The Kosovo Albanians, and especially the KLA, objected because the proposal did not give them independence. It did not rule it out, though. The key paragraph read in part:

> Three years after the entry into force of the agreement an international meeting shall be convened to determine a mechanism for a final settlement for Kosovo, on the basis of the will of the people, opinions of relevant authorities, each of the Party's

efforts regarding the implementation of this Agreement, and the Helsinki Final Act.[6]

Madeleine Albright made clear to the Kosovars that she understood "will of the people" to mean a referendum, which, given the structure of Kosovo's population, obviously meant independence. However, the Helsinki Final Act also talks of the territorial integrity of states. Thaçi was under huge pressure from the KLA on the ground and grandees such as Adem Demaçi not to sign. Albright's memoirs on how she tackled the recalcitrant Thaçi are revealing in their brutal honesty:

> I tried a variety of tactics. First I told Thaçi what a great potential leader he was. When that didn't work, I said we were disappointed in him, that if he thought we would bomb the Serbs even if the Albanians rejected the agreement, he was wrong. We could never get NATO support for that. "On the other hand," I said, "if you say yes and the Serbs say no, NATO will strike and go on striking until Serb forces are out and NATO can go in. You will have security. And you will be able to govern yourselves."[7]

For the Albanians the situation was saved by Surroi, who devised a formula by which they said they would sign the document—but only after consultations back home and in two weeks.

When the two sides returned to Paris on March 15 Thaçi announced that he was happy to sign. The Serbs, however, came back with an almost entirely new proposal. They had crossed out roughly half of the original, for example the bit about Kosovo's future being decided by the "will of the people," and had replaced these parts with their own ideas.

It was too late. Some 2,000 had already died in the conflict and, while, never mentioned explicitly, a ghost haunted the proceedings, or rather the leaders of all of the major Western powers. It was, as noted earlier, the massacre of more than 7,000 Bosniaks after the fall of Srebrenica. The guilt that this engendered was a major factor in propelling Bill Clinton, Tony Blair, and the other Western leaders to take action now. If such a crime had happened before, there was no guarantee that it might not happen again. The fact that no explicit UN Security Council resolution endorsed the 78 days of bombing that were now to begin should be understood in that political context.

The bombing began on March 24. A few days earlier the UNHCR reported that there were already some 250,000 displaced within Kosovo because of the fighting. More Serbian forces were now moving into Kosovo, and as the KVM pulled out, another 25,000 were in flight from Drenica. One of the main reasons given by Western leaders for the intervention was to prevent a humanitarian catastrophe.

Very soon it became clear that both sides had miscalculated. Western leaders had believed that the bombing would be short-lived. After all, it had taken only a few days of bombing to help propel the Serbs to Dayton in 1995. They believed the conflict would not last long. Milošević therefore also thought he could take the risk. He also believed he would get serious help, including perhaps military help from Russia. He did not.

For the next 78 days Serbia, Kosovo, and some targets in Montenegro were subject to major aerial bombardment. Military targets were hit, targets that were perceived as having a "dual use," as well as factories and other places where the Yugoslav army and security forces had withdrawn to hide equipment and facilities. The military proved themselves to be masters of dissimulation, making large numbers of fake targets—for example, tanks made out of plywood—which attracted fire. They also hid among civilians and in civilian areas. Within Kosovo the KLA was rapidly reduced to near impotence, although it held some small areas, including some on the border. Several massacres helped propel hundreds of thousands to flee. Serbian policy toward the Kosovo Albanians was confused, or, rather, varied to such an extent that it is hard to work out any pattern.

At the end of March, tens of thousands of Albanians from two districts of Pristina were rounded up and deported at gunpoint, by train, to Macedonia. Many more fled but after this there were no more clearances from Pristina. Albanians were expelled from Peć/Peja and the old town of Djakovica/ Gjakova was torched and people deported. In some areas, people were assembled to leave and marched or driven around Kosovo before being sent home. In some rural areas people were effectively herded from scattered hamlets into smaller, more concentrated areas and then deported or simply abandoned. Serbian paramilitaries, many of whom consisted of men released from prison on the condition they serve, rampaged across the countryside killing, looting, and torching homes. By the time the bombing had ended, the UNHCR reported that 848,100 Albanians had fled the province. Of these, 444,600 were in Albania, 244,500 in Macedonia, 69,000 in Montenegro, and 91,057 in other countries.[8] Including the hundreds of thousands displaced within Kosovo, some 1.45 million Kosovo Albanians were displaced.[9]

One of Milošević's war aims appears to have been to take advantage of the bombing and to get rid of as many Albanians as possible from Kosovo. At the border many were stripped of their documents, which would have made it hard for them to return in the event of a ceasefire and Serbia remaining in control of the province. He also perhaps hoped to spread the conflict to Macedonia at the very least, by inflaming passions between the country's own Albanians and Macedonians. This failed, not the least because NATO quickly moved to contain the situation by building camps for the refugees on the border. In terms of world support, the first few days of the conflict were bad for NATO, for Serbia was able to portray itself as an innocent victim of NATO aggression, merely trying to safeguard its territorial integrity. This argument was rapidly drowned out by the images of the hundreds of thousands of Albanians in flight.

In general terms the NATO bombing was mostly accurate, though hundreds of civilians, both Serbs and Albanians, were killed and thousands were wounded. Most military targets and buildings, such as the General Staff building in the center of Belgrade, were empty when hit. NATO had no interest in killing large numbers of people in these buildings and warnings appear to have been sent about what sort of targets were in NATO's sights.

But mistakes happened. In Serbia, for example, cluster bombs hit civilians in the city of Niš on May 7, causing 14 civilian deaths, and a train was bombed on the Grdelica Bridge, close to Leskovac, on April 12. There were several accidents like this: according to the U.S. group Human Rights Watch, which carried out extensive research, an estimated 500 civilians died in 90 separate incidents.[10] Ironically, a large number of them were Kosovo Albanians who may have been used in columns along the road as human shields by Serbian forces. On May 13, for example, somewhere between 48 and 87 died in an attack near the village of Koriša/Korisha, where the refugees had stopped. One of the worst single massacres by Serbian forces was of between 345 and 377 Albanian men (and some boys) from surrounding areas, murdered in the village of Meja on April 27. Afterward, just before NATO entered Kosovo, many of the bodies were exhumed, and with hundreds of others—some 836 in total—reburied in the Batajnica air base near Belgrade and two other places.[11]

One month later, Milošević and four others were indicted by the UN's Yugoslav war crimes tribunal in The Hague for what had happened in Kosovo, including the Meja and Racak/Reçak massacres and the forced deportation of more than 800,000 Albanians. Serbs thought that this was proof that the tribunal was simply a political tool of Western leaders. In fact Louise Arbour, the chief prosecutor, rushed to indict the Serbian leader out of fear that as part of the deal to end the war he might negotiate some form of immunity. Milošević, who fell from power on October 5, 2000, was eventually to die on March 11, 2003, in custody in The Hague during his trial.

The bombing of Yugoslavia ended on June 10, 1999. In the end, after weeks of hard bargaining, especially between the Russians and the Americans, Milošević was presented with a fait accompli. On June 3 he was visited by Victor Chernomyrdin, a former Russian prime minister, and Martti Ahtisaari, a former Finnish president, who had been picked to represent Western countries. By now Milošević understood that Russia was in no position to help. He may also have understood that if he gave in now Russian troops would attempt to carve out a sector in postwar Kosovo in the Serbian-inhabited north, which could then be used as a possible future step toward partition. Serious discussions had also begun among the NATO allies about the possible need for a ground war. Finally, Milošević had failed to spread the war to Macedonia; attempts to persuade the Bosnian Serbs to rebel had also fallen on deaf ears.

Under the terms of the deal, which was to be enshrined in Security Council Resolution 1244, which was passed on June 10, Serbian forces were to withdraw from Kosovo and to be replaced by a NATO-led force and a UN administration. Some Serbian forces would be allowed to return later to maintain a presence at Serbian "patrimonial" sites and to maintain a presence at key border crossings. This would never happen, for KFOR, the NATO-led Kosovo force that was now moving in to Kosovo, would never deem the region safe enough for them to return. In the wake of the resolution, and as Serb forces pulled out of Kosovo and the administration there collapsed, Milošević proclaimed that Serbia and Yugoslavia had won a magnificent victory. Russia was thwarted in its attempts to have its own sector in Kosovo. NATO troops entered on June 12, soon followed by hundreds of thousands of refugees eager to return home. The war is generally estimated to have cost some 10,000 lives in Kosovo.

In the general euphoria that followed, many did not see, or overlooked, the dreadful reprisals that took place against Serbs in particular but also against Roma and other non-Albanians. NATO troops were unprepared to deal with the murders and mayhem that accompanied their arrival in the province and the flight of tens of thousands of Serbs, accompanied by attacks on Orthodox churches. This was a particularly shameful episode. In one incident alone, on July 23, 14 men harvesting in the fields in Staro Gracko/Gracko e Vjetër were murdered. Serb and Roma houses, and those of other non-Albanians, were burned. A report prepared by the OSCE noted (typically) that a "keynote feature" of immediate post-conflict Prizren was house-burning.

In the town they have nearly exclusively been Kosovo Serbian properties burned with the obvious intention of preventing returns, but they have also been used to signal to the international community and the moderate part of the Kosovo Albanian population who is in control. The overall result is that far more damage has been caused in Prizren town after the war than during it.... By the end of October, nearly 300 houses have been burned in Prizren and the surrounding villages. The result of this pressure on the Kosovo Serbs is clear: 97 percent of the pre-war population have left.[12]

The only really significant Kosovo Albanian to stand up and protest about this was Surroi, for which he earned death threats. In the next few months Serbs left virtually all towns in Kosovo and in most places elsewhere retreated into enclaves such as Gračanica/Graçanica, Štrpce/Shtërpca, and Goraždevac/Gorazhdevc. For many years, but depending on where they lived, freedom of movement was difficult, but it became much easier in the latter years of the UN period.

Almost nine years after the end of the war, Carla Del Ponte, the former chief prosecutor of the UN's war crimes tribunal in The Hague, said in a book published in Italy that she had received credible reports, with compelling circumstantial evidence, that soon after NATO arrived in Kosovo some 300 Kosovo Serbs were abducted and taken to Albania, and that some of them were murdered after organs had been taken from their bodies to sell. No bodies were found, however. The tribunal could not proceed due to jurisdictional limitations and a lack of further leads, and neither the future UNMIK nor the Kosovo or Albanian authorities carried the investigation further. The Swiss foreign ministry subsequently banned Del Ponte, Switzerland's ambassador to Argentina, from promoting the book.

9

KOSOVO AFTER 1999

It is impossible to underestimate the chaos of Kosovo in the wake of the war. Albanians streamed back in and Serbs fled, or were ethnically cleansed, from their homes and villages. Some 120,000 houses had either been destroyed or damaged and bridges and other key infrastructure bombed. Most significant, however, was the collapse of any law and order. As the administration of Kosovo had been in Serbian hands, it simply vanished, or rather, it vanished from those parts of Kosovo where Albanians lived, which was of course most of it.

In this chaotic period it was unclear what was happening in this regard, but as the dust cleared so did the situation. Parts of the Serbian local administration collapsed entirely, some continued to function in some Serbian areas—particularly in the north—and some departments withdrew to become kinds of offices in exile to Serbia. Meanwhile, in the first weeks after the end of the war the KLA attempted to seize local power and to fill the vacuum, and in this it was mostly successful. Nonetheless it must certainly also be regarded as a huge success of the incoming UN administration that eventually it managed to displace the KLA and replace it, not only with its own personnel but, after the first local elections in October

2000, with elected officials, too. Some of these were the same people, but at least this time around they were elected.

Under the terms of Security Council Resolution 1244, jurisdiction in Kosovo passed to the UN, which in turn created the United Nations Interim Administration Mission in Kosovo (UNMIK). The resolution had been aimed at ending the bombing, so it was contradictory and, in keys parts, unclear. For example, it states clearly on the one hand that it reaffirms the "sovereignty and territorial integrity of the Federal Republic of Yugoslavia" (of which Serbia was, after 2006, its legal successor) but on the other also demands that full account be taken of the Rambouillet accords, which in turn speak of determining a final settlement "on the basis of the will of the people."

In the meantime, however, it was clear(ish) on what UNMIK had to do: help rebuild Kosovo and provide it with a "transitional administration while establishing and overseeing the development of provisional democratic self-governing institutions to ensure conditions for a peaceful and normal life for all inhabitants of Kosovo."[1] Under the UNMIK structure, four so-called pillars were created. One of them, dealing with refugees, was headed by the UNHCR but this was phased out by June 2000. After a reorganization in May 2001, Pillars One and Two comprising civil administration, police, and justice were run directly by UNMIK, while economic reconstruction was under the jurisdiction of the EU and institution building assigned to the OSCE. At the top of UNMIK was the Special Representative of the Secretary General, who was always known as the SRSG.

At the moment of the declaration of independence in 2008, UNMIK appeared very much like a tired organization that had outlived its usefulness. Some staff had become tainted by corruption and it was uncertain what more UNMIK could do. However, despite criticism within Kosovo and from abroad, UNMIK managed to achieve a lot. In effect it fulfilled its mandate of helping to create Kosovo's institutions and giving its people the means to live as much of an ordinary life as possible. Key accomplishments included the creation and training of the Kosovo Police Service (KPS), giving people documents such as UNMIK passports, and overseeing the creation of an assembly, a government, and so on. In June 1999 Kosovo had no police. By November 2007 it had 7,124 officers, of whom 6,082 were Albanians, 746 were Serbs, and 414 were from other groups.[2] This was a success, although in the wake of independence KPS began to split along ethnic grounds. One real problem was its inability to deal with crime if the criminals were powerful and politically well connected. Such issues are not unique to Kosovo or the Western Balkans, of course.[3]

Several key dates need to be noted. In January 2000, UNMIK initiated what were in effect proto ministries, which were headed by both a foreigner and a local. In May 2001, a constitutional framework was adopted that was to lead to general elections, the creation of an assembly, a government, and the presidency. From then on, power was gradually ceded to Kosovo's institutions (with some exceptions: for example, in the field of foreign affairs). Final say about anything, however, remained, if necessary, with the SRSG. As Kosovo's security was assured by KFOR, and Resolution 1244 called for the disarmament of the KLA, this was done under pressure but by means of a neat trick. The KLA was disbanded, but several thousand of its men were absorbed into the so-called Kosovo Protection Corps (KPC), which was supposed only to be a civil defense force, helping out in case of emergencies, such as forest fires and people being cut off by snow. However, it was widely understood to be a Kosovo army in waiting.

It would be easy to get lost in the myriad details of who did what during the UNMIK years. Its first, flamboyant, proper head was Bernard Kouchner, the French politician who was one of the founders of Médecins Sans Frontières. Kouchner was a passionate believer in liberal interventionism and, after the election of Nicolas Sarkozy as president of France in May 2007, foreign minister. Five more SRSGs followed until the declaration of independence in 2008, none of whom had his panache, and one or two of whom accomplished little. By 2008, however, it was possible to make some sort of assessment of the UNMIK years.

Veton Surroi takes a sanguine and balanced view. UNMIK, he says, was, "a bridge between oppression and the future independent state. It allowed for the institutions to be built from scratch to get to the situation in which we are now." Surroi also believes that Kouchner played a hugely important role during his term from July 1999 to January 2001, a period when tensions ran high, not just with Serbs but between Albanians, that is to say between those who had supported the KLA and supporters of the reemerging LDK under Rugova. He had gone into exile during the war and subsequently returned only to find himself, much to his own surprise perhaps, still extraordinarily popular. "If we had not had that political and military authority," says Surroi, referring to UNMIK and KFOR, he believes that Kosovo could even have descended into civil war. It was during this period that several LDK activists were assassinated.

Agim Çeku, who commanded the KLA in the latter stages of the war, then was head of the KPC and later prime minister, thinks that this assessment goes too far. But he, too, stresses the extraordinary difference between Kosovo in 2008 and in 1999. "We are thankful for that. They rebuilt this society and they did well." Where Çeku sees failings are in areas which, at the beginning, seemed like small problems that could be and were initially disregarded, but that now loom large. These include, for example, illegal building, which is rife in Kosovo. "For two or three years no one cared about that but now it has become a habit and a big problem." In the end however, says Surroi, UNMIK ran up against philosophical buffers:

> There was an internal paradox in the UN mission. It was here to build a democratic society and the basic precondition of that is the rule of law. But if the UN is the supreme law it does not allow a society of the rule of law because it is the final authority. The SRSG can pass any law, because he is the final authority. So, you have a kind of postmodern neocolonial power.

On the eve of transition from the UNMIK years to what looked set to be the era of the EU protectorate, Surroi's fear was that the duality of power created by UNMIK, that is, that between the government it had created and its own power, would continue into the new era in which the watchword above all would be stability rather than democracy. Thus Kosovo would become a state captive to the demand of the international community for quiet above all in disorderly places. That being case, he feared discreet trade-offs being made by Kosovo Albanian leaders and foreigners sent to Kosovo to help run the place.

Unfortunately, especially in a book such as this, readers should be aware that there are also many things that are either known or widely believed but which cannot be written about for legal reasons. The sort of thing being referred to includes questions of when outsiders turn a blind eye to things they should not, in return for stability. In Kosovo, journalists can get killed for probing into these things so, in general, they don't. Ivan Krastev, the prominent Bulgarian social scientist, noted, talking about the Balkans in general, "The border between organized crime and the state is the least-guarded border in the Balkans." While acknowledging this, however, and the fact that drugs, prostitutes, petrol, and other contraband have been smuggled into and through Kosovo over the years, it is also important not to exaggerate the significance of this phenomenon, or, rather, to single out Kosovo with particular regard to organized crime, which is frequently done in the propaganda wars.

One of the most striking things about Kosovo after 1999 was how rapidly its physical and mental geography changed. During the 1990s, Serbia and the Serbs were physically very prominent in Kosovo through the use of the Cyrillic alphabet, flags, documents, police, administration, radio, television, and so on. All of that vanished rapidly in Albanian-majority areas. Or rather, it all simply changed. Serbian flags were replaced with Albanian ones. The Yugoslav dinar was replaced first with the German mark and then with the euro. Serbian printed media vanished.

And of course, so did Serbs. Many left because they were frightened, many because they did not want to live in an Albanian-dominated territory, and many because they were simply intimidated out of their flats, in Pristina and elsewhere, by Albanians who wanted them. Especially at the beginning, murders were common, but these declined to virtually none by 2007, in part because Serbs and Albanians had more or less physically separated and because Albanians understood that violence risked putting their national cause in jeopardy.

Basically, most but not all of Kosovo became Albanian. The issue of Serbian enclaves will be addressed, but some more points need to be made here about everyday life.

Serbian rule in most of Kosovo came to an end and, as we have seen during the UNMIK years, a new reality was created. But anomalies could not be avoided, and these things affected people in the most mundane ways. Serbia remained nominally sovereign. In our world, sovereignty and its myriad manifestations are something we do not really think about. Take phone calls. The old Yugoslav international dialing code was +381. After the breakup of the first Yugoslavia, and the final divorce of Montenegro and Serbia, the latter retained this, unlike the other parts of the old Yugoslavia, which acquired their own numbers. Except for Kosovo, of course, which, not being a state, was stuck with it. Cell phones were different. In 1999 Kosovo was covered by the Serbian network, whose prefix is 063. The new Kosovo needed its own cell phone network but it was not going to use +381. Thus it managed to borrow the presumably underused prefix +377, which belongs to Monaco. For some years 063 persisted in much of the territory but was later forced to retreat to Serbian areas. Kosovo's authorities regarded 063 as illegal, especially as the network paid no taxes in Kosovo, but as the Serbs relied on it, it survived. Any attempt to switch off its base stations was interpreted as an attack on Serbs. But the symbolism of the result was huge. If a Kosovo Albanian wanted to call his Serbian friend up the road, he was making an international call, that is, from Kosovo's network to Serbia's. In 2007 Kosovo got a second network, which was Slovene owned. Now Kosovo had another international code, that of Slovenia, but still none of it its own.

What was true of cell phones was also true of identification papers. As the Serbs had taken documents from people as they fled in 1999, many had no passports or identity cards. Over time UNMIK was to issue them, but at first people who needed to travel had to get Yugoslav passports. The travel documents issued by UNMIK were, at the time of independence, only accepted by 39 countries. Serbia continued to demand Serbian documents from any Kosovars who needed to travel through Serbia.[4] Over the years, then, hundreds of thousands of documents and passports were issued to Albanians by Serbia, which of course argued that they were entitled to them because they were citizens of Serbia. As for cars, UNMIK devised a number plate with the letters "KS" in the middle, which would be the same for Albanians and for Serbs, even if the latter used Cyrillic letters. The neutral plates helped Serbs especially, enabling them to drive around without fear. But Serbia refused to accept these and so you could not drive your car into Serbia with them. Instead you had to pay for temporary plates or—as many Serbs did—get both Serbian Kosovo plates and KS plates. Over the years people learned to juggle with such problems, but it marked them as Europeans who could not live as other Europeans did, with services provided by the state that could be taken for granted.

During the months after the end of the war Kosovo's big towns rapidly emptied of almost all Serbs, and it was widely assumed that soon there would be none left. Serbia claimed initially that there were some 230,000 displaced people from Kosovo, the vast majority being Serbs, of course, but including 37,000 Roma, too. Later this went up to more than 280,000.[5] However, it became clear that actually not all of the Serbs had left. Instead, there appeared to be quite a lot remaining.

In the immediate aftermath of the war, French soldiers took control of Mitrovica. It had always been mixed but what happened now was that Serbs left the south and most, but not all Albanians, left, or rather did not return to the north, and so the town was quickly divided at the River Ibar/Ibër. From there to the Serbian border the region has traditionally been Serbian-inhabited, with few Albanians. At the northern end of the bridge dividing the town, Serbs sat in the Dolce Vita Café, keeping an eye out in case of trouble coming from the Albanian south. They were called the Bridge Watchers. On one side of the bridge everyone spoke Albanian, used euros, KS plates, and Kosovo cell phones, and looked to their leaders in Pristina. On the other, people spoke Serbian, used dinars (as well as euros), Serbian number plates, Serbian phone networks, and Serbian papers.

While KFOR did establish itself in the north, UNMIK never really did. Its officials talked of "parallel institutions" but really they were Serbian government ones, either directly or indirectly, via institutions that were now created for Kosovo, such as the Serbian National Council or the Serbian government's Coordination Center. De facto, the north remained under Serbian control. If Kosovo was ever to be formally partitioned, then the Ibar would be the border.

The problem was that most Kosovo Serbs were not in the north. At first the figure put forth by Serbia of 230,000 displaced was a mystery. How could it be so large when the 1991 census, taken while Serbs were in control, showed that there were only 214,235 Serbs and Montenegrins in Kosovo? Now there were *more* than that number in Serbia, with another 100,000 or more remaining in Kosovo?[6] The answer, it seems, was that even though UNHCR had adopted the Serbian figure, it was not true.

In 2004 the Berlin-based think tank, the European Stability Initiative (ESI), conducted the first serious research into this question. Gerald Knaus, the director of ESI, said that five years after the end of the war he was stunned by all sorts of official documents in and about Kosovo in which the numbers of Kosovo Serbs and Albanians varied enormously, making any kind of serious planning, including everything from education and health care to decentralization, a hit-and-miss affair.

And yet, he explained, making an accurate assessment was not necessarily hard to do. ESI based their estimate of Serbs in Kosovo on the easily available figures of primary school enrollments. Their results showed that "there are still nearly 130,000 Serbs living in Kosovo today, representing two-thirds of the pre-war Serb population." Of these, it said that almost two-thirds (75,000) lived south of the Ibar, that is, in enclaves surrounded by Albanian areas, or in mixed villages. "Almost all of the urban Serbs have left," said the report, "with North Mitrovica now the last remaining urban outpost. However, most rural Serbs have never left their homes. The reality of Kosovo Serbs today is small communities of subsistence farmers scattered widely across Kosovo."[7] The exception to this was western Kosovo, where even most rural Serbs had left. After the report was published, and in the wake of the violence of March of 2004, more Serbs, especially younger ones might have subsequently left, but still it put the issue in stark perspective.

Today, Serbs live in larger enclaves, such as Gračanica/ Graçanica and a string of villages around Pristina, Štrpce/ Shtërpca, and many smaller ones, such Goraždevac/ Gorazh-devc in the west, and then in mixed villages around Gnjilane/ Gjilan. Security varied over time and by place. Goraždevac near Peć/Peja was one of the worst places. On August 13, 2003, two young Serbs were killed and four injured when fired at from across the river they were swimming in. Some 1,000 people lived here. There was hardly any work, and to move in and out of the village people had to wait for a twice-weekly escort of KFOR peacekeepers. A war memorial commemorates locals killed by "Albanian terrorists" and NATO bombs. One man explained: "If Kosovo gets its independence what would we wait for? We'd all go. There would be nothing to wait for."

In fact, many Serbs did not stay in Kosovo only because they had nowhere else to go. A large but unknown number stayed because they received double salaries from Belgrade—for example, for teachers, medical staff, and other civil servants. For some years these turned into triple salaries as, until ordered not to do so by Belgrade, many of these people also got paid by the Kosovo government. How many stay in the wake of independence will be directly related to whether this money continues to flow. In the immediate aftermath it appeared not only that it would but that there would be cash for those who had not been on the payroll before.[8] This issue also clouded the question of how many Serbs there were, given that some of them commuted between family in Serbia and jobs in Kosovo. Over the years, a huge investment was made attempting to lure Serbs who had fled back to Kosovo. The Serbian government always made a point of this issue, but in general terms it was a failure. Between 2001 and 2007 some 17,821 "minority returns" were registered.[9] However it is uncertain how many of these people actually stayed rather than pretending to return in order to take advantage of various financial incentives. Some also returned and then left again after the violence of March 2004.

What was never said clearly, however, was nonetheless obvious. The vast majority of Serbs who had left did not want to live in an Albanian-dominated state, just as Albanians did not want to live in a Serbian state. Since most Kosovo Serbs did not speak Albanian, opportunities would clearly be limited, especially for young people, who generally did not want to eke out their lives as subsistence farmers.

Because of its nature, the Kosovo story is always presented as one of Serbs and Albanians. But, after 1999, Serbs were probably only half, or perhaps 60 percent, of the total number of non-Albanians in Kosovo. The rest were a hodge-podge of other minorities. The biggest single one is composed of local, Serbian-speaking Slav Muslims, many of whom since 1999 have chosen to identify themselves as Bosniaks, or Bosnian Muslims. A large number live in and around Prizren. Then come Roma, some of whom are called Ashkali and some of whom "Egyptians" (to which the word "gypsy" may be related, of course), then Turks, then another Slav Muslim group called "Gorani," and then a tiny number of Croats, the vast majority of whom had been leaving since the early 1990s to resettle in places in Croatia from which the Serbs had in turn fled. In the wake of the war, many Roma fled or were ethnically cleansed because Albanians believed them to be Serbian collaborators.

Goranis, too, found themselves in a difficult position. They live in one of the most beautiful if isolated parts of Kosovo—around and south of the town of Dragaš/Dragash in the Gora region, which is a mountainous peninsula south of Prizren, hemmed in to the east by Macedonia and to the west by Albania. Their language is something between Serbian and Macedonian, though in school they have always learned in Serbian, and many of them were loyal Serbian citizens, serving in the police and as officials until the end of the war. Before the war there were anywhere up to 18,000 of them, but by the end of 2006 their own leaders estimated that only 8,000 of them remained. Hamdije Seapi, a local official in the village of Mlike, said that before the war there were 1,380 people in the village, but now there were barely 400, of whom 70 percent were over the age of 65. "Before we were somehow like shock absorbers between Serbs and Albanians," he said, "but now we have our backs to the walls."

Everyone in Kosovo will remember the UNMIK years for different reasons. But for many its biggest failing was the economy. Perhaps expectations were too great. After all, Kosovo had never been self-sustaining even in the old Yugoslavia. For decades large amounts of money poured into the province from richer parts of the country, especially Slovenia and Croatia, who increasingly came to resent this. Kosovo is also small but then Kosovars, both Albanians and Serbs, had the option of working elsewhere in Yugoslavia and as *gastarbeiters* (guest workers) elsewhere in Europe. Despite this, Kosovo always remained one of the poorest parts of the country. It did get richer, but what rankled was that other parts got much richer still, so the gap between say Kosovo and Slovenia was constantly widening. Kosovo Albanians claim that this was due less the population explosion than to enduring a kind of colonial experience. For example, selling raw materials, especially from the Trepča mines, at fixed, not world, prices, to the Slovenes, who got rich by selling them washing machines made from those materials in return.

Kosovo's economy went into a tailspin during the 1990s, but after 1999 experienced a temporary boom, thanks to reconstruction and the influx of tens of thousands of soldiers, UN staff, and other foreigners. Additionally, there was a huge amount of international largesse. According to the IMF, five billion euros had been spent in Kosovo by 2005 (although half of that was allocated to international salaries).[10] "With a per capita income of €1,300," noted an April 2008 report by the think tank the Kosovo Stability Initiative (IKS), "Kosovo is an island of poverty in Europe."

With only 54 percent of the working age population economically active, Kosovo has the lowest labour force participation rate in Europe. Subsistence agriculture is still the largest employer; 85 percent of food produced in Kosovo never makes it to the market. 45 percent of the population in Kosovo lives below the poverty line, on less than €1.4 a day. Registered unemployment has been increasing relentlessly and an additional 30,000 youngsters press onto the labour market every year. Economic growth in the range of 3.1 percent, as forecast by the Ministry of Finance and Economy is nowhere near enough to begin absorbing the existing unemployed.[11]

All of this is true but can be misleading unless understood in context. Kosovo looks and feels like a poor part of Europe—but not the Third World. Family solidarity is strong and the vast majority of families own their own homes. Remittances from family abroad are also a huge source of income, though how much that is remains unclear, given that much of that money has always come in people's pockets and thus is impossible really to quantify. Nevertheless, IKS note that in 2002 the Ministry of Finance did make an attempt. They estimated that "of Kosovo's total income of €1,570 million, €720 million came from cash remittances. At its peak, foreign assistance and private inflows in the form of savings and remittances accounted for nearly half of Kosovo's GDP."[12] *Gastarbeiter* pensions are also a huge but unknown source of income for large numbers of people. Someone who had a relatively modest job for some 20 years in Switzerland, for example, could expect to receive a monthly income of €2,500. It is in this context that the above figure of €1.4 a day needs to be understood. If most people really *only* lived on that, then life would not just be hard for everyone but most people in Kosovo would be starving to death.

10

MARCH 2004 AND THE AHTISAARI PLAN

The UN years can be divided neatly in two: before March 17, 2004, and after. Beginning in December 2003, the major plank of UNMIK and international policy was called Standards before Status. Its aim was to put off questions about Kosovo's final status for as long as possible, while still setting European standards for Kosovo's government, known in official jargon as the Provisional Institutions of Self-Government (PISG). "The Standards for Kosovo are a set of targets that Kosovo must meet in order for the talks about the future political status of Kosovo to begin," said the UN.[1]

After March 17, when Kosovo was convulsed by an unexpected spasm of violence, rioting, and pogroms, the policy changed. It was clear that it was no longer sustainable. Kai Eide, a top Norwegian diplomat with considerable experience of the Balkans and Kosovo, was asked by the UN to prepare a report in which he indicated that it was time to start talks between Serbs and Albanians on the future. This began the process that was to lead to the plan for Kosovo prepared under the leadership of Martti Ahtisaari, the former Finnish president who had been involved in the talks to end NATO's bombing of Yugoslavia.

The "standards" that Kosovo was supposed to live up to before any move to discussing status were developed over the period 2002–2003. According to UNMIK, they were designed "to create a fairer and more tolerant society, and improve levels of public sector performance." They covered eight fields within which 109 goals were identified. The eight fields were: functioning democratic institutions, rule of law, freedom of movement, sustainable returns and the rights of communities and their members, economy, property rights (including cultural heritage), Pristina-Belgrade dialogue, and the Kosovo Protection Corps.[2]

All sorts of complex measures were worked out to see if Kosovo was attaining the standards, and they were useful in the sense that they gave a guide to all concerned about what they were supposed to be doing and aiming at. Kosovo Albanians grumbled, though, saying that no other country was required to reach such high standards. Serbs, by contrast, argued that Kosovo was always falling short and that it would therefore be a very long time before there was any point in talking about status. After the March riots, the standards mutated to Standards with Status, and then were more or less forgotten.

The March events began in Čaglavica/Çagllavica, a suburb of Pristina that straddles the main road to Skopje. In the past it used to be a mainly Serbian area and many Serb houses sat along the road. On the evening of March 15 a Serb from Čaglavica was seriously wounded by assailants he claimed were Albanians. The next day, in protest, Serbs in Čaglavica blocked the main road and also cut the road to Gnjilane/Gjilan, which runs through the adjacent Serbian enclave of Gračanica. On the same day KLA veterans associations, along with those of the families of people still missing from the war, held angry rallies across Kosovo to protest the arrest by UNMIK police of four former KLA commanders for war crimes.[3] That afternoon the Albanian-language media began reporting that three Albanian children had been drowned while fleeing Serbs in the River Ibër. The next day all hell broke loose. Albanians clashed with Serbs in Çagllavica, and in Mitrovica with the Albanians, whipped up by a media that appeared to have lost control, especially in laying blame for the deaths of the boys. Subsequent investigations could find no proof of the story that they had been chased into the river by Serbs, but the damage had been done.[4]

UNMIK and KFOR were taken unawares and were slow to react, while what might have begun as general protests soon appeared not only to be gaining momentum, but to be directed by shadowy groups or individuals. Kosovo's leaders, with the exception of the prime minister Bajram Rexhepi, also seemed reluctant to condemn what was going on, or were at best half-hearted. Vulnerable Serbs and Roma came under attack. Houses, schools, and health centers were torched. Orthodox churches also came under attack, including some medieval ones, as did UNMIK cars and buildings.

By the time the violence subsided, 19 people were dead, 11 Albanians and 8 Serbs. Nine hundred were injured, and 29 Serbian churches and monasteries were set on fire or otherwise damaged. By March 24 the UN was reporting that some 4,366 people had been forced to flee. About 360 of them were Albanians and a similar number were Romas. The rest were Serbs.

The two days of rioting sent shock waves across Kosovo and the region, but even more important, it sent shock waves through the UN and foreign ministries concerned with the region. After various inquiries, in May 2005 Kofi Annan, the

UN secretary general, appointed Kai Eide, then Norway's ambassador to NATO, to conduct a mission. He was asked whether or not it was time to begin talks on the final, or at least future status of the province. In his frank 16-page assessment, which was presented to Kofi Annan in October, Ambassador Eide said that progress in implementing the UN standards was "uneven." He wrote, "Regrettably, little has been achieved to create a foundation for a multi-ethnic society. Kosovo's leaders and the international community should take urgent steps in order to correct this grim picture." However he went on to point out: "There will not be any good moment for addressing Kosovo's future status...nevertheless an overall assessment leads to the conclusion that the time has come to commence this process."[5]

In response to the Eide report, in November 2005 Kofi Annan asked Martti Ahtisaari to oversee talks on the future of Kosovo. These took place in Vienna and in general proved desultory and inconclusive. Unsurprisingly, Serbia and the Kosovo Albanians could not agree on the all-important final status of the territory, that is, whether it should be independent or not. Serbia's policy platform was that Kosovo could have "more than independence but less than autonomy," and the Albanians were willing to give the Serbs almost anything, so long as they agreed to independence. From the very beginning, albeit in private, Ahtisaari was clear that he believed that independence was the only way forward. By contrast, the Serbs felt, correctly, that if and when the issue of independence ever came to the Security Council they could rely on Russia. So, to a great extent, neither side had much of an incentive to find a historic compromise.

In the end, following 14 months of talks, Ahtisaari and his team drew up their own plan, which in many key respects had

Ethnic Populations, 2008 (*Map by Phil Kenny*)

been foreshadowed by Eide's report and suggestions. Given that the north and the Serbian enclaves were de facto run by, or at least heavily influenced by, Serbia, the core of the plan was decentralization, understood as code for Serbian autonomy. The plan foresaw that these areas should be allowed to have special links, including financial, with Serbia. Areas around important Orthodox churches and monasteries would also have a special status. What Ahtisaari was trying to do was to find a legal and better formula for a situation that in many ways already existed but to move it forward within the context of an independent Kosovo.

Foreseeing problems with the Russians, Ahtisaari did not use the word *independence* within the body of the plan. However, in a covering report, he talked about "supervised independence." There he added that since Serbs and Albanians had "diametrically opposed positions...no amount of additional talks, whatever the format, will overcome this impasse." His conclusion was that "the only viable option for Kosovo is independence, to be supervised for an initial period by the international community."[6]

Under the terms of Ahtisaari's plan, NATO-led troops would stay in Kosovo but supervision of the new state would pass out of the hands of the UN, whose mission would leave 120 days after the passing of a Security Council resolution "endorsing" or "supporting" it. Although international officials at the time and subsequently said that Kosovars would be running their own new state, in fact a large amount of power was to remain reserved for outsiders. Two new organizations were foreseen to exercise this power, both of which began to deploy after Kosovo declared independence. The context for that was rather different from the way it had been envisaged by Ahtisaari, though. His plan was presented to the

Security Council on March 26, 2007, where Russia successfully blocked it.

The two connected organizations were an EU mission and a smaller one called the International Civilian Office (ICO). They would both be deployed as European Security and Defense Policy (ESDP) missions. The first was finally endorsed by all EU states on February 16, 2008, one day before the declaration of independence, and called EULEX, drawing on the Latin word for "law." Under the terms of the Ahtisaari proposal, which had also been backed in 2007 by all EU members, its job was to "monitor, mentor and advise on all areas related to the rule of law in Kosovo. It shall have the right to investigate and prosecute independently sensitive crimes, such as organized crime, inter-ethnic crime, financial crime, and war crimes." Including policemen, the mission was to comprise some 1,900 internationals and 1,100 locals. While this mission would clearly be important, even more so would be the far smaller ICO, headed by an International Civilian Representative (ICR).

The first ICR arrived in Kosovo two days after the declaration of independence to begin his mission: Pieter Feith, a distinguished Dutch diplomat who had experience in Macedonia and then in Aceh, in Indonesia, where he had helped implement a settlement for the breakaway province, also crafted by Ahtisaari. Feith was "double-hatted" as the EU's Special Representative (EUSR). Technically he was to oversee "the implementation of a status settlement and act as EUSR when offering the EU's advice and support in the political process as well as in promoting overall EU coordination and coherence in Kosovo, including in the area of rule of law."[7] These lines (including the ones on EULEX above) are taken from the Ahtisaari report and produced in the EU's glossy leaflets, which explained to people what the EU and Feith would be doing. What the leaflets did not say but what the plan also said is significant. The ICR, it said,

> shall have no direct role in the administration of Kosovo, but shall have strong corrective powers to ensure the successful implementation of the Settlement. Among his/her powers is the ability to annul decisions or laws adopted by Kosovo authorities and sanction and remove public officials whose actions he/she determines to be inconsistent with the Settlement.[8]

Two points need to be made. The Settlement is of course Ahtisaari's plan. But the plan was never endorsed by the Security Council. So, in effect, a deal was made with the Kosovo Albanians: they would get recognition from the bulk of EU states and support, including money, so long as they incorporated the main provisions of the plan into their law, which they did, and also invite in both missions. Behind both the Kosovo Albanians and the EU stood the United States, whom the Albanians trusted more because of their consistent and staunch support since Rambouillet. The Americans were not only encouraging but also very likely assisted in writing the declaration of independence, which said: "We accept fully the obligations for Kosovo contained in the Ahtisaari Plan, and we welcome the framework it proposes to guide Kosovo in the years ahead. We shall implement in full those obligations...particularly those that promote and protect the rights of communities and their members."[9]

The second point is that few realized just how powerful the ICR would be, at least if he exercised his power. The ICR was modeled on the post of High Representative in Bosnia and Hercegovina, who also had virtually governor-general–like powers (although there they were called the "Bonn Powers"). So, at the dawn of independence, Kosovo did not look as though it would be quite as independent as its people expected. The years of the UN protectorate looked as though they were giving way to those of something entirely new: an EU protectorate—at least in those areas where Albanians lived.

11
KOSOVO AND THE REGION

Sometimes on the graves of Kosovo Albanian fighters, on Albanian Internet sites, and elsewhere you see an unfamiliar map, one that engulfs and dwarfs Kosovo. It is Greater or, as Albanians like to call it, "ethnic Albania." The question it raises is whether the independence of Kosovo is just the first step toward the creation of a Greater Albania or whether Albanians, who have lived separately for so long now, will be content to continue to do so, rather like German speakers in Switzerland, Germany, and Austria.

Before the demise of the Ottoman Empire, Albanians were divided among four *vilayets,* or administrative regions. These were Shkodër, Janina, Monastir, and Kosovo. (The first is called "Skadar" in Serbian or Montenegrin, the second "Ioannina" in Greek, and the town of Monastir is known today as "Bitola" in Macedonian.) Their borders were not static and changed over the years. The first encompassed much of what is now northern Albania and the second much of southern Albania and also a lot of what is now northern Greece. Monastir took in a large part of Macedonia and also central Albania. Kosovo was the largest of them all, and it covered most of what is now the Sandžak region of Serbia, including Novi Pazar,

Skopje in Macedonia, and parts of modern Bulgaria. While the concentrations of Albanians varied enormously by region, one reason they were split and mixed with large numbers of Christians and Slavs was because the Ottomans did not want to encourage the emergence of any strong Albanian region. Geography—mountains and a lack of roads and communications—also helped keep Albanians divided and thus weak.

This division, and the ambivalence felt by at least Muslim Albanians toward the Ottoman Empire, meant, as we have already seen, that compared to their Orthodox neighbors, Serbs and Greeks especially, Albanians were late when it came to developing a modern national identity. Even more important, as the empire was gradually chipped away and finally collapsed, Albanians had no small state to mobilize to try and unite all of their compatriots in one country. The Albanian state that was proclaimed in 1912 encompassed only half or so of the Albanians of the Balkans. It is not surprising, then, that in 1915 most Albanians in Kosovo welcomed the short-lived demise of Serbian rule, as they did the creation of a Greater Albania in 1941.

The reimposition of Yugoslav rule after the Second World War did not mean that Albanians ceased to dream that one day they might be united in one country, however remote such an idea might have seemed. The development of a Kosovo Albanian middle class and intellectuals also played a key role in promoting a national idea, especially as they continually underscored the fact that Albanians were not Slavs. This was a key consideration in the adoption in 1972 of a standard literary Albanian based on the Tosk dialect of southern Albania, from where Enver Hoxha and the novelist Ismail Kadare came from. And yet, something else was happening in parallel to this, especially once Albania became a hermit-like, sealed country that few could visit, and the cry went up for a Kosovo republic. A distinct identity began to develop in Kosovo itself, one that was more than simply geographic. The question today is to what extent that identity has developed, and whether Kosovo Albanians feel themselves to be Albanian for sure, but also Kosovar as something else.

During the 1990s, when the old Yugoslavia collapsed, Serbs and Croats, respectively, sought to create a Greater Serbia and Greater Croatia. Now most Serbs, and many others, too, are convinced that because this is what *they* wanted it is only a matter of time before Albanians demand the creation of a Greater Albania. Logic suggests they should be right, but evidence, if one sets aside the demands of a fringe of hard-line nationalists, suggests that this may not be the case. Since the demise of communism, in neither Kosovo nor Albania have political parties advocating the union of the two ever made serious headway. A poll in Kosovo in 2005 found that while 90.2 percent supported an independent state, only 9.1 percent supported union with Albania.[1] This suggests something Albanian nationalists hate: that over the last 20 years many, especially younger Albanians in Kosovo, have developed a new Kosovar identity. It does not mean they do not feel Albanian, but simply they do not feel a contradiction in feeling Kosovar, too.

Over the last few years debate about this has intensified, especially because Kosovo, until the day of the declaration of independence, did not have its own flag (the red banner with the double-headed eagle, which all Albanians regard as their own, is, of course, also the flag of Albania). An independent Kosovo needed its own. Prominent in this debate over identity has been Migjen Kelmendi, who edits *Java*, a paper

written (controversially) in Gheg, Kosovo's own Albanian
dialect, as opposed to standard Albanian. He says that when
Kosovo was oppressed by Serbia "I had to identify with
Albanianism." Now, much to the anger of an older generation,
including Ismail Kadare, he feels relaxed and proud about
being a Kosovar as well as an Albanian.

This is the legacy of the difference between the other peoples
of the former Yugoslavia and the Kosovo Albanians. Until
1991, virtually all Serbs and Croats lived in one country, while
Albanians did not. Thus, since 1912, they have grown apart.
Politicians in Albania, who have plenty of their own everyday
problems to grapple with, have never shown much interest in
Albanians outside of Albania. Now Kosovo Albanian leaders
have every intention of enjoying their independence and no
wish to submerge their new state and their power into that of
another.

Albanian nationalists hate the expression "Greater Albania"
and prefer to talk about "ethnic Albania." This refers to an area
that is much smaller than that covered by the four Ottoman
vilayets, but it certainly takes in, apart from Albania and
Kosovo, western Macedonia, the Albanian-inhabited districts
of southern Serbia, and parts of northern Greece (Çamëria),
which historically had a native Albanian population. As
with other such nationalists, the fact that there are many
non-Albanians in these regions is just ignored. In that sense
Albanian nationalists believe in the same thing as do others
across the region: "Why should I be a minority in your state if
you can be a minority in mine?"

Most Albanians, wherever they are, are generally uninter-
ested in creating a new state on all of this land, if only because
they believe it is unrealistic. Remzi Lani, an astute political
analyst from Tirana, summed up the view from Albania thus:

"If I said there were no people who dreamed of a Greater Albania I would be wrong. But it is not a popular idea. If the Security Council or an international conference offered us a Greater Albania we would not refuse it, but on the other hand we are not going to fight for it either."

Of course views will vary across the region and, for example, the Albanians of south Serbia will have very different views and priorities from Albanians in southern Albania, but in general terms joining the EU and creating a greater level of prosperity is what concerns them more. By contrast, what does happen, especially between Kosovo and Macedonia, is that politicians and academics, students, businessmen, and criminals all move as if they do already (or still) live in one country. Ali Ahmeti, for example, was a founder of the KLA, although he was born in Kičevo in Macedonia. During the brief 2001 conflict in Macedonia he was the head of the Albanian guerrillas there and he is now the head of one of the country's two main Albanian political parties. If it was realistic, many Macedonian Albanians might well opt to become part of a Greater Kosovo, but given that this is not on the agenda, it is simply not a live issue. During the conflict of 2001 Adelina Marku, who used to be a spokeswoman for an Albanian party in Macedonia and comes from Debar in the west of country, put it this way. Debar is close to the Albanian border, and, when asked if people there would like to see a Greater Albania, she replied, "Of course they want that," but then she added that her people had to "face reality." It was, she said, "too late for that, so what is important now is to make borders unimportant."

Within Macedonia, however, invisible borders are becoming more apparent. The last two decades have seen the phenomenon of the winnowing out of the Macedonians and Macedonian Albanians. Areas that used to be mixed are ever less so, and thus Albanian areas are ever more compact. Mentally tuned to a larger Albanian world, especially thanks to television, the Internet, and the media in general, Albanians and Macedonians, while able to get on with one another, have less to do with each other than ever. If, one day, borders are redrawn in the Balkans, then that will be easier now in Macedonia than it once might have been.

Albanians know that talk of a Greater Albania scares the rest of the region and Europe, and, as in Kosovo, many Albanian politicians in Macedonia would rather be large fish in a small pond than small fish in a large one. Given the realities of the region, one Macedonian Albanian politician, Teuta Arifi, argues that Albanians should follow the example of German speakers, whom she notes have "built various identities in Germany, Switzerland and Austria while they continue to belong to the same German culture."[2] This seems to be happening already. Indeed a pan-Albanian cultural and economic space is emerging, albeit slowly. Bookshops in Kosovo are full of books from Albania, and Kosovars watch Albanian television (though not vice versa because Albanians from Albania say programs from Kosovo are boring).

In terms of business, however, there is a long way to go. In 2005 Kosovo's exports to Albania amounted to a mere €48 million, and Albania did not even rank among the top ten countries from which it imported a total of €1.1 billion.[3] In a potential pan-Albanian market of more than 6 million consumers, only insurance appears to have made any real headway. Likewise, Kosovo ranks very low as an Albanian trading partner, despite a 2003 bilateral and now regional free trade agreement.[4] One of the main reasons for this is that neither Kosovo nor Albania actually produce very much, and certainly not much of interest to each other, but over the years, this may change, especially as local purchasing power increases. Where there is the possibility of a genuine market, it can flourish quickly. Kosovars and Macedonian Albanians increasingly take their holidays in Albania now, and hotels, restaurants, and other infrastructure have been rapidly created to cater for their needs—most dramatically in Vlore.

In the run-up to independence in Kosovo, moderate Kosovo Albanian leaders argued that the only things Kosovars wanted were independence within the borders they had inherited from Yugoslavia and European integration, which would make these borders unimportant. It would not matter that there was a Serbian north of Kosovo or Albanians in south Serbia or western Macedonia, and so on. It is too early to say what will happen, but it has long been clear that the fate of northern Kosovo and the Preševo/Presheva Valley are linked. That is to say, there would be no reason Albanians should accept that the Preševo region should stay trouble-free and integrated into Serbia, were Serbia the de facto power in both northern Kosovo and the Serbian enclaves. This story remains to be played out but it connects directly to Macedonia and Bosnia-Hercegovina, too. On March 17, 2008, when violence broke out in North Mitrovica, Veton Surroi was asked whether the effective loss of northern Kosovo to Serbia would provoke reactions among Albanians elsewhere. He replied, "With such developments as we are seeing now in the north I think it is highly probable... that we will hear increasingly voices of people who want ethnic settlements by redrawing borders and unfortunately I would not exclude violent behaviour to do so."[5]

Indeed, one reason so many have been reticent about Kosovo's independence is the fear of what may follow. Since Kosovo was only a province of Serbia what makes it different from the Republika Srpska (RS), the Serb part of Bosnia? This is a legitimate question, and in 2007 and 2008 was one frequently raised in Bosnia and Serbia, especially by Vojislav Kostunica, the Serbian prime minister who linked the two areas, as did Milorad Dodik, the powerful prime minister of the RS. Serbs have argued that were Kosovo's Albanians allowed an independent state on the basis of a right to national self-determination and, for example, if a referendum on independence for the RS was ever held and the question of its union with Serbia put on the table, then by what right could that be denied? In January 2008 Dodik said that in upcoming talks on constitutional reform in Bosnia his party would demand a right to self-determination including the option of secession.

Within Bosnia this argument is explosive because it leads right back to the causes of the war in 1992. Bosniaks retort that the RS is not a legitimate entity; it is based on genocide and ethnic cleansing, and thus the aim should be to abolish it altogether and to create a unified Bosnian state. But, argue Serbs, this is exactly what Serbs objected to in the first place: that a Bosnian state of citizens, as opposed to one of Bosniaks, Croats, and Serbs, would in reality be one dominated by Bosniaks who are the largest of its three peoples. "Republika Srpska does not have the right to secede," from Bosnia, said Miroslav Lajcak, the international community's High Representative, a kind of modern-day governor-generalship. Bosnia, he said, "is an internationally recognized state, its territorial integrity is guaranteed by the Dayton Peace Agreement and its existence cannot be questioned."[6] Lajcak is not just the High Representative but also the EU's Special Representative in Bosnia. So, Serbs argue, it is one law for Albanians and one law for Serbs. No wonder Kosovo is regarded as the problem from hell in Brussels, headquarters of the EU.

Within Bosnia, since the war, a huge amount of progress has been made in rebuilding a country decent enough for all of its citizens to live in. However, most ordinary Serbs and Croats still regard Serbia and Croatia as their motherlands. They watch Serbian and Croatian television, go more to Zagreb and Belgrade than Sarajevo, send their children to university in those countries, and support them, not Bosnia, in international football matches. This is one of the legacies of the Balkan wars of the 1990s and it has a direct connection with Kosovo today. That is to say, we know what the questions are, we know what the landscape is, but we do not know how the issue will develop. For example, will Serbian areas in Kosovo eventually become like Serbian parts of Bosnia, where the population is unenthusiastic about the state they live in but does not really have much to do with it? Will Serbian, Albanian, and other leaders in the region accept that many of their compatriots must live outside of the motherland?

Time will tell. Several scenarios are possible. One is that the current de facto partition continues, with UNMIK remaining in Serbian but not in Albanian areas. The second is that the effective loss of northern Kosovo provokes a reexamination of the Albanian question. That is to say, those in favor of unification with Albania gain ground arguing that since an independent Kosovo within its existing borders, progressing peacefully on the road to European integration, has not proved possible, Albanians need to find another path. In that case, of course, as Surroi indicated above, all bets on the future stability of the Balkans and its borders are off.

Another possibility is that after some, or many, years of uncomfortable coexistence, Serbs and Albanians decide to talk seriously about redrawing their borders, which would also have ramifications in Bosnia and Macedonia. Indeed, although they are a minority, there are those, in the region and abroad, who argue that today we are in an illogical situation: we are attempting to force people to live within the confines of borders drawn in a different time and for different circumstances and that a conference, harking back to the 1878 Congress of Berlin, which redrew the map of the Balkans in the wake of the Russo-Turkish War, should be called to reexamine and redraw Balkan frontiers. One eloquent exponent of this line of thought is Thanos Veremis, the vice president of ELIAMEP, Greece's most influential think tank. He argues that the majority of the citizens of Bosnia would like the "peaceful dissolution of their segregated state" and that if Kosovo's Albanians have gained independence owing to their right of self-determination, then this is a "powerful medicine which should be applied equitably."[7]

The problem is that if the powers that be conceded that you could, and even should, redraw the borders of the Balkans, which could never be done to everyone's satisfaction, this would simply open the Pandora's box of all disputed borders across the planet.

12

KOSOVO AND THE WORLD

Kosovo is small. Its territory covers 6,759 square miles (10,887 square kilometers). By way of comparison, Connecticut is 8,920 square miles (14,356 square kilometers), and Wales is 12,911 square miles (20,779 square kilometers). Lebanon is marginally smaller than Kosovo, and Jamaica is 64 square miles (104 square kilometers) larger. Even by regional standards Kosovo is small. Albania covers 17,863 square miles (28,748 square kilometers), Macedonia 15,977 square miles (25,713 square kilometers), and even Montenegro, which is often dubbed "tiny," is almost one-third larger.

In terms of world politics, though, size doesn't matter. Geography does, and so do geopolitics. Israel is twice the size of Kosovo but the West Bank and Gaza are only two-thirds the size of Kosovo. Rwanda is a little larger than Israel, and Western Sahara has been occupied by Morocco since 1975, despite a judgment from the UN's International Court of Justice that it possessed the right of self-determination. Nobody said that the world was a fair place.

In Kosovo's case, apart from geography, there is also the issue of precedent. Or, depending on your point of view, maybe not. When wondering why anyone in the outside world cares about Kosovo or the Western Balkans in general, the answer is simple. As noted at the beginning of this book, look at the map. Kosovo and the Western Balkans are not on the periphery of Europe, they are bang in the middle. When Bulgaria and Romania both joined NATO in 2004 and then the EU in 2007, a European circle was closed—right around Kosovo and the rest of the region. This is what is often known as the Balkan Ghetto. If Kosovo lay on the further reaches of the Black Sea, then policy makers in EU countries and the United States would be far less concerned by what happened there. Abkhazia, which broke away from Georgia in the early 1990s, has by comparison, been almost completely ignored by the EU.

Being in a ghetto has several implications. The first is that while containment is a possible policy, in the long run it is self-defeating. A restrictive visa policy, for example, has meant that ordinary people who want to visit the rest of Europe become embittered, while the criminals, among others that such a policy is designed to keep out, never have a problem procuring the necessary papers. In Thessalonika in 2003 the EU made a commitment to all of the Western Balkan countries that, one day, they should all be members.

This was not entirely a gesture of European brotherly love. Indeed it comes with a stiff dose of self-interest: if Kosovo and the region can be made "more like us," with efficient functioning states, abiding by the rule of law, they are less likely to go back to war, cause outflows of refugees, need thousands of peacekeepers to pacify them, or be the source of large numbers of illegal migrants, many of whom by virtue of being illegal are forced into a life of crime. The mechanism for putting the Western Balkan states on track to the EU is called a Stabilization and Association Agreement (SAA). This is the

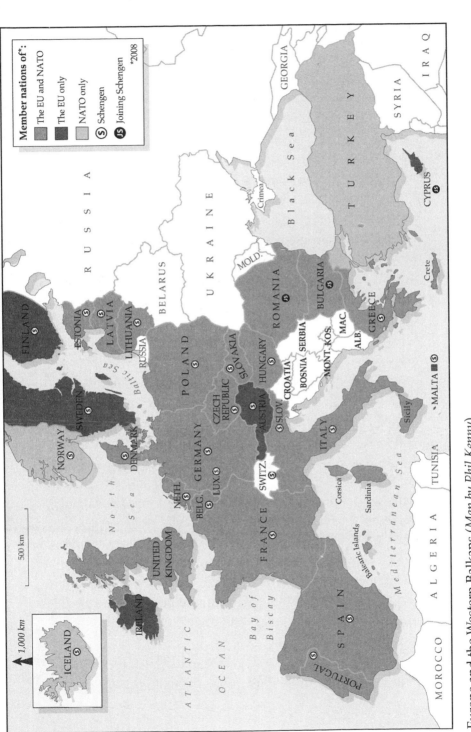

Europe and the Western Balkans (*Map by Phil Kenny*)

first contractual agreement with the EU. After this the country becomes a formal candidate, like Croatia and Macedonia, and then opens negotiations. Kosovo, not being a state, of course, until it declared independence, was put on a special system called a Tracking Mechanism, to help prepare it for an eventual SAA. Since there was no precedent for Kosovo, there was no precedent for this either.

But "precedent" is what has always concerned the diplomats, strategists, and lawyers about Kosovo. The question has been whether its independence would set one for other separatist territories. First, we need to remind ourselves about what made Kosovo different from the other parts of Yugoslavia. When the country was reconstituted after the Second World War it was re-created as a federal state and, as noted, the Kosovo Albanians, the majority of the population, had no say in whether they desired this or not—because, of course, they did not. Over the years and through various mutations and constitutions the six Yugoslav republics gained ever more power. Kosovo was not a republic, however, but after a period as an autonomous region in 1963 it was promoted to become an autonomous province like Vojvodina, Serbia's northern region.

Yugoslavia, then, bears comparison with the other two communist federations that dissolved: Czechoslovakia and the Soviet Union. When both of them collapsed they did so along the lines of their constituent parts, that is to say the Czech and Slovak republics and the 15 Soviet republics. Unlike Czechoslovakia, many of the Soviet republics contained various autonomous regions and republics. Today, Russia contains 21 such republics, including Chechnya, Tatarstan, and North Ossetia-Alania.

In 1991, as Yugoslavia was disintegrating, the then European Community (now the European Union) asked Robert

Badinter, a distinguished French constitutional lawyer, to head a commission to which it could turn for advice. Its most important conclusion was that Yugoslavia had dissolved into its republican parts, which could be recognized as new states. What this meant was that Serbs as a whole and as a nation did not have the right to self-determination, which would have meant redrawing the borders of the republics, which is of course exactly what the Serbs under Milošević wanted to do. Badinter's commission was not asked about Kosovo but, by implication, because it was part of Serbia, it did not have the right to statehood like Croatia, Bosnia, and the other parts of Yugoslavia. At the time Kosovo was quiet and what the Europeans and others concerned with managing the crisis wanted to avoid was drawing new frontiers. Kosovo Albanians argued that, in fact, although theirs was not a republic, it had all the same rights and thus, as they were not seeking to redraw *their* borders, they had a right to independence too.

This is the problem that has bedeviled Kosovo ever since. The Russians, for example argue that Kosovo's independence might set a precedent for any separatist-minded unit of a former Soviet republic, not to mention other parts of the world. And they have a point. Why should Kosovars be allowed independence but not Chechens? For now, Chechnya is back under Russian control, but what about ten years hence? Pavel Felgenhauer, a leading Russian commentator, has argued that

the threat of a disintegrating Russia—comparable to the break-up of the Soviet Union in 1991—is still today seen as a very real threat by the Kremlin and the Russian elite.... The West is seen today by many in the Russian elite and public as a threatening force that is plotting to tear Russia apart and

rob it of its natural resources. By supporting Serbia's right to
veto Kosovo's secession…the Kremlin clearly believes that it
is defending Russia's undisputed right to sustain its territorial
integrity by any means available.[1]

Outside of Russia itself but within the area of the former Soviet
Union, four places, or "frozen conflicts," are often mentioned
with respect to Kosovo and the precedent issue: Transnistria,
which has broken away from Moldova; the Armenian populated region of Nagorno-Karabakh, which has broken away
from Azerbaijan; and Abkhazia and South Ossetia, which
have both declared independence from Georgia.

It is often argued that Kosovo is a unique case, or sui generis,
to use the jargon favored by lawyers. This argument is just as
commonly rejected. "If people in Kosovo can be granted full
independence," asked Vladimir Putin, then Russia's president, "why then should we deny it to Abkhazia and South
Ossetia?"[2] On the face of it, he might have a good case, but
then once you look at the places in question you see quite how
different they are. Take Abkhazia, on the Black Sea. Before its
conflict, which took place in the early 1990s, only 17.8 percent
of its population was Abkhaz. Today, of some 200,000 people,
they still only constitute 45 percent of its people, and more
than 200,000 Georgian refugees from Abkhazia want to return
home. The Abkhaz, who are in firm control of the government and of all levers of power, argue that to allow more to
come back than they have already permitted would simply
be to turn back the clock and to make them once more just
a small minority in their own homeland. Ironically, while
Russia supports Abkhazia, if not its full independence, and it
has opposed Kosovo's independence, that does not mean that
the Abkhaz are against it. "Just because Russia does not want

Kosovo to be recognized," says Maxim Gunjia, the deputy foreign minister of Abkhazia, "it does not mean that we do not want it."

The same is true in South Ossetia. "Those rules which work for Kosovo will work for South Ossetia," says Alan Pliev, its deputy foreign minister, in Tskhinvali, the muddy, village-like capital of South Ossetia whose main thoroughfare is called "Stalin Street." But South Ossetia has a tiny population— anywhere between 22,000, as the Georgians claim, and 70,000, according to the South Ossetians. It is hardly a candidate to be a viable state, especially as large swaths of it are held by the Georgians, but perhaps that is not the aim. South Ossetia is connected to Russia by a tunnel through the mountains. On the other side lies the autonomous republic of North Ossetia. "Our aim is unification with North Ossetia," says Alan Pliev. "We don't know if that would be as part of Russia or as a separate united Ossetian state." Juri Dzittsojty, deputy speaker of parliament, says: "I would prefer there to be an independent and united Ossetia, but today it is not possible. It is safer to be with Russia. The main aim of the struggle is to be independent of Georgia."

While the Russians and Serbs argue that Kosovo's independence would be precedent setting, one thing that is noticeable is the extent to which Russia could be argued to have set a precedent for Kosovo. The Abkhaz and South Ossetians are officially Georgian citizens, but almost all have Russian passports and vote in Russian elections. Russia supports the separatists financially, too, and pays pensions in these territories, which also use the ruble. In that sense a precedent, or at least an example, was set by Russia, which has been followed, albeit in a rather different context, by Serbia in its support of the Kosovo Serbs.

Across the world there are scores of separatist or poten- tially separatist regions. They range from Tibet, to the Basque country, to Flanders, Quebec, and Taiwan. Quite apart from the legal issue, which pits the territorial integrity of the state against that of a nation's right to self-determination, there is the political context to consider. Does the independence of Kosovo really embolden separatists everywhere, or is that a red herring? Would the slight legal difference that distinguished it from say, the former Yugoslav republic of Montenegro, which was warmly welcomed by the rest of the world as an independent state in 2006, and which has three times fewer people, really make waves in Canada or China? When Tibet exploded in violence a month after Kosovo declared indepen- dence, were any Tibetans really aware of Kosovo and what had happened there a month earlier?

Quite apart from the legal and precedent issue, Kosovo, despite its diminutive size, has become a key test for the EU's declared Common Foreign and Security Policy (CFSP), of which European Security and Defense Policy (ESDP) is a part. The former aims to define the general outlines and principles of EU foreign policy and to formulate common strategies. ESDP aims to give CFSP common capabilities in the political, civilian, and military fields. Since its launch in 1999, there have been several ESDP missions around the world. Most of them have been relatively modest in scale, though with time they have been increasing in ambition. In 2004, some 6,000 EU-led troops took over peacekeeping operations in Bosnia from NATO. In January 2008, the green light was given for a 3,700-strong force for Chad, to deal with overspill from the war in Darfur, and on February 16, 2008, EULEX for Kosovo was approved. As noted earlier, the mission called for the deploy- ment of 1,900 international policemen, judges, prosecutors, and customs officials plus 1,100 locals. Although the basics of law and order in Kosovo were of course to be taken care of by the government, the powers given to the mission indicated the self-interest of the EU—in this case in having an active role to play in those issues that (in the field of organized crime and trafficking, for example) directly impact member states. In Bosnia, the EU's troops, run down to 2,500 in 2007, never faced a challenge. But the success or failure of the mission in Kosovo will be a major test for the EU and its ability to project power to protect its interests by, at the same time, promoting those of others, in this case those of the people of Kosovo.

In terms of CFSP, Kosovo was a relative success, at least until Kosovo declared independence. In mid-2007, EU states were divided over the issue. However, we need to examine the context in which a Kosovo policy was formed. Throughout 2007 Britain and France favored following the United States in recognizing the new state when the time came, while Germany was ambivalent. One of the main reasons Germany had broken with the United States over the invasion of Iraq in 2003 was the fact that it had not been sanctioned by the UN. Other countries were also unconvinced of the merits of recognizing Kosovo. Mostly they were countries that had potential or real separatist problems of their own—Cyprus being the most obvious. Slovakia and Romania worried about their Hungarian minorities, while Spain was uncomfortable because of Basque and Catalan separatist tendencies. This began to shift in the latter half of 2007, in great measure due to Russia.

In 2006, Western diplomats were firmly convinced that while Russia would be uncomfortable with Kosovo's independence they would still go along with it. After all, they argued, when NATO went to war with the Serbs in 1999, the Russians had complained, but actually done nothing. Their argument ran that the Russians were happy to use the Serbs, but would always betray them in the end.

As Ahtisaari presided over his talks in Vienna, European and American diplomats kept asking their counterparts in Moscow what they wanted in exchange for allowing the Security Council to bless Kosovo's independence. When the Russians were unforthcoming—refusing to name their price, something to do with energy, perhaps; or maybe Iran or the United States' proposed missile-defense shield—Western diplomats chuckled that the Russians were just being shrewd traders, ready at the last minute to strike the best deal possible for the highest price.

Still, not everyone was convinced. "I told my colleagues that this time the Russians were serious and they meant it," says a senior EU diplomat from a former communist country, "but they just said, 'we know what we are doing.'" On March 26, 2007, Ahtisaari's plan was presented to the Security Council. Now the Russians *had* to make a deal thought the diplomats, otherwise there would be a real mess. "As you know we can only support a draft resolution that is acceptable to both sides, Pristina and Belgrade," said Russia's foreign minister Sergei Lavrov on July 12, using the coded language which meant "no deal."[3]

Several draft resolutions were penned, and the Russians said "nyet" to all of them, since they all basically endorsed the Ahtisaari's plan and thus foresaw independence. "Almost the entire text," said Vitaly Churkin, Russia's UN ambassador, of one draft, "is permeated with the concept of the independence of Kosovo," noting that the chances of its being adopted as it was were "zero."[4] There were two immediate reasons for this. First, the Russians suspected that any resolution which did not reiterate Resolution 1244's assertion of the territorial integrity of Serbia would be used to justify the later recognition of an independent state, and second, the Russians were indeed right that the draft was a way of getting Kosovo to independence by stealth. On July 20 the game was over. There were to be no more attempts in the Security Council to find a formulation of words that would have endorsed the Ahtisaari Plan and hence independence for Kosovo.

By now it was becoming much clearer why the Russians were not looking for a deal. It was not because the diplomats who had at the beginning of the process thought that Russia was being difficult because it wanted respect as a Great Power and wanted to be involved in the process were wrong. It was because between the beginning of the process and the end Russia had changed, and this had happened so fast that they had not noticed. Well, Kosovo was a good way of making them take notice. For Russia, of course, the issue was not about Kosovo as such, but rather about several other things. There was the precedent issue discussed above; there was also Moscow demanding the respect it had lost in the wake of the collapse of the Soviet Union. But there was something else here, too. For many of the leading figures involved, such as Churkin and Lavrov, it was personal. During the 1999 bombing of Yugoslavia, for example, Lavrov had been Russia's ambassador at the UN. Now was the time to seek revenge on Western countries for what Russians perceive as their humiliation in the 1990s, epitomized by the bombing that they could not prevent. Indeed Sergei Karaganov, a political advisor to the Putin administration, said as much when he commented on June 16, "Many in Moscow now want American and European colleagues to pay the full price for their games in Kosovo, although they do not want to admit it publicly."[5]

So, on the geopolitical world stage, Kosovo was a small but useful pawn. Victor Yasmann, in a comment for Radio Free Europe, noted that Kosovo was a "weak link" in Western policy. "Russia realizes that any unilateral declaration of independence for Kosovo that does not follow UN procedure will not be recognized by all members of the European Union, and could cause a rift within the bloc."[6] As if to underline this and to cause consternation in the EU, Putin, speaking at an energy summit on June 24 in Zagreb, the Croatian capital, said that the Balkans had always been a "sphere" of Russian "special interest" and that it was "natural that a resurgent Russia is returning there."[7] This came soon after President George Bush, speaking about Kosovo in Tirana on June 10, had told ecstatic Albanians "We need to get to moving…and the end result is independence."[8]

There is no one reason why a resurgent Russia decided to make use of Kosovo. There are several, all of them important for different reasons and for different people. But if one of the aims was to use Kosovo to help keep the EU divided, the policy had mixed results. After Russia blocked a new Security Council resolution on Kosovo, a diplomatic troika was set up to see if there was any possibility at all of striking a deal between Serbs and Albanians. It consisted of one ambassador each from the United States, Russia, and the EU. The Russians wanted it to become a stepping stone to endless negotiations, effectively freezing the situation, which is also what Serbia wanted. The troika was given 120 days to do its work, which, predictably, led nowhere. Or not quite. In fact, the 120 days were exactly what the EU needed to build what its diplomats called the "critical mass": enough EU states ready to recognize Kosovo when the time came, and to make sure that all 27 countries were behind the ESDP mission.

And that's where we come to CFSP—and Russia's contribution. Russia's policy on Kosovo began to appear as something aggressive that needed to be countered. The EU had, as a whole, supported the Ahtisaari plan, but here was Russia telling its members that they could not do what they wanted in their own inner courtyard. It was enough to swing Germany. If Germany was certain to support independence now, then so was Italy, and then so were most EU states, if not all straightaway. The diehard exception was Cyprus, which, along with Greece, was now being labeled by the think tank the European Council on Foreign Relations as Russia's Trojan horses within the EU.[9] But the two of them on their own were not enough to prevent the creation of a policy that now, however reluctantly, foresaw that Kosovo's independence was inevitable, and that it was in the EU's best interests to manage the transition from the UN, as well as to support the fledgling state in its early years with EULEX and the ICO, even if all states did not immediately recognize the new state, a fact that undeniably dented the cause of the union's CFSP.

13

NOT THE LAST CHAPTER: INDEPENDENCE

Kosovo's Albanians declared independence on February 17, 2008. On the eve, one European diplomat who had played a key role in developments in Kosovo over the past couple of years sighed that he had mixed feelings about what was about to happen. It was, he agreed, not the longed-for "final status" that the Kosovo Albanians wanted, nor was it a solution that was clear, which was what the diplomats wanted. It was thus not the last chapter in the story that had begun in 1999 (or 1989, or 1912, or 1389...), but rather just a new chapter. "We had hoped we'd be finishing the book by now," he said.

The run-up to the declaration began toward the end of 2007. The troika mission was doomed from the start in the sense that everyone knew that there would be no break-through "historic compromise" between Serbs and Albanians. The latter had no incentive to negotiate anything short of independence, as U.S. officials were clear that as far they were concerned that was the only realistic solution, and they knew that the main EU countries agreed. Likewise the Serbs knew that Russia would back them, not recognize Kosovo, declare its independence illegal, and block Kosovo's entrance to the UN, making it a state, less than equal with all others. In this it was backed by several other major countries, including China.

Ban Ki-moon, the UN secretary general, had asked the troika to report to him by December 10, and many fixed on this date as though something might actually happen on it. The government in Pristina bought fireworks to be ready for the declaration of independence. As the date approached, however, a joke began to do the rounds. To the question "What comes after December 10th?" the reply was, "December 11th." And so it proved to be. In the event, the troika had so little to say that they handed in their report several days early. Foreign journalists descended on Kosovo, believing that something was about to happen, and when it did not, disappointed perhaps, many wrote alarmist reports about the upcoming new Balkan war. Such hyped reporting ignored the fundamental changes that had taken place in the Western Balkans since the fall of Slobodan Milošević on October 5, 2000. That aside, it was clear that the region was in for a period of turbulence and perhaps even spasms of violence.

The period from December 10 to February 17 was taken up with fierce lobbying by the Serbian government, led by Vojislav Koštunica, the nationalist prime minister, and Boris Tadić, the pro-European president, both of whom of course opposed independence. To recognize Kosovo as an independent state, they said, would violate international law and commit a great injustice against Serbs. Further, Serbia would never recognize it.

Kosovo itself had held elections in November of 2007 and Hashim Thaçi was its new prime minister. He had a reputation of having evolved considerably since his days as the political commander of the KLA. He knew when to say the right things, to make conciliatory gestures toward Serbs, and he was believed to listen very carefully to advice that came first and foremost from the United States. Almost to the end, the Kosovo Albanians felt jittery that something could go wrong, but Thaçi and others became ever bolder in their statements that independence was coming soon. It was now, they insisted, not a question of a unilateral declaration so much as a "coordinated" declaration—that is to say coordinated with their friends in Washington, Brussels, and elsewhere.

In essence a deal was done. Kosovo would declare independence but had to agree to implement the Ahtisaari Plan, or it least incorporate it into its law and invite in the ICO and EULEX. It also had to acknowledge that Resolution 1244 stayed in place, because no resolution had been passed to replace it. What this would mean in practice was not immediately clear. A final part of the deal was that the Kosovo Albanians were asked, or told, to wait until after Serbia's presidential election was over. Boris Tadić faced a strong challenge from Tomislav Nikolić, the leader of the hard-line nationalist Serbian Radical Party, whose founder, Vojislav Šešelj, was on trial at the UN's war crimes tribunal in The Hague.

Tadić won on February 3 with 51 percent of the vote to Nikolić's 49 percent. Tadić's message was that, whatever happened in Kosovo, Serbia had no choice but to pursue European integration. Nikolić, along with Koštunica, who was at the same time in coalition with Tadić's party, argued that you could not continue with European integration if the EU decided to deploy EULEX, which they said would be illegal. They did not wish to join the EU if the bulk of EU states recognized what they now took to calling the future "fake," "phony," or "NATO" state.

In the days running up to the declaration, one could hardly tell that something momentous was about to happen. The reason, explained Agron Bajrami, the editor of the daily *Koha Ditore*, was that there had been so many disappointments in the past that people would only begin to celebrate when it actually happened. Kosovo Serbs were either nervous or defiant. In the north, few were worried but, especially in the smaller of the enclaves, others were. In Gojbulja, for example, 4.3 miles (7 kilometers) south of Mitrovica, home to a shrinking community of some 250 Serbs, bored, disconsolate men sat in a smoky shop cum bar watching Serbian television. They were worried that if demonstrations by Serbs in North Mitrovica turned nasty and Albanians were chased, either from the Bošnjačka Mahala part of the town where some lived or the few other Albanian settlements in northern Kosovo, they would be the first targets of revenge. Bratislav Kostić, Gojbulja's Serbian leader, lamented that while national leaders had been saying that Kosovo Serbs should simply ignore any declaration, they had received no instructions from anyone about what to do.

Until virtually 48 hours before the declaration there was some doubt that it would actually happen on February 17. Even when Hashim Thaçi addressed a packed press conference two days before the big day he refused to be drawn on the date, although he pledged to look after Kosovo's minorities. It was a moment pregnant with symbolism. Since no one had bothered to provide a translation, none of the now-angry Serbian journalists had a clue what he was saying.

Celebrations finally began on the afternoon of February 16. It was bitterly cold. Cars began driving round the center of Pristina packed with excited youths waving flags. The next day, parliament was called to meet at 3:00 PM. No Serb deputies were present, most of them having absented themselves from Kosovo. They had all been elected with a tiny number of votes anyway, as almost all Serbs had, on the instructions of the government in Belgrade, boycotted the polls. Ten seats are specially reserved in parliament for Serbs. Three asked the speaker beforehand if they could speak, but he said they could not, and, anyway, no deputies would be allowed to speak. They then said they were withdrawing from parliament.

The ceremonies were presided over by Thaçi. The declaration was passed unanimously by 109 deputies. Despite the bitter cold, thousands celebrated in the center of Pristina. Free beer and water were distributed, and a massive cake was quickly gobbled up by anyone who could get near it. Groups danced in the street and paraded with Albanian flags, which were everywhere. Some had managed to get hold of Kosovo's new flag—the map of Kosovo set on a background of European blue plus six stars, which were said to represent six ethnic communities in Kosovo.[1] Lots of American flags were waved, and many European ones, too. There were no untoward incidents. That night, Pristina was treated to a fireworks display the likes of which had never been seen before.

The declaration itself was enlightening. Many suspected that the Albanians had some help, or even a lot of help, in writing it from their foreign friends, especially in the United States. The word "Albanian" did not appear in the text. It read: "We declare Kosovo to be a democratic, secular and multiethnic republic, guided by the principles of non-discrimination and equal protection under the law. We shall protect and promote the rights of all communities in Kosovo and create the conditions necessary for their effective participation in political and decision-making processes."[2]

Significantly, and as per the deal worked out with the Americans and the main European states supporting independence, the declaration also read, "We accept fully the obligations for Kosovo contained in the Ahtisaari Plan." It added, "We shall act consistent with principles of international law and resolutions of the Security Council of the United Nations, including Resolution 1244." It also read, "We invite and welcome an international civilian presence to supervise our implementation of the Ahtisaari Plan, and a European Union-led rule of law mission."[3] That referred to the ICO and EULEX. All of this was confusing. It was unclear as to who was actually going to be in control. According to Resolution 1244, the SRSG was the boss. If Kosovo was independent, the last word on governing the country should lie with the members of its elected government, but, on the other hand, the declaration welcomed the ICO, whose head could, should he see fit, sack them.

Kosovo Albanians celebrated for a few more days before life returned to normal. Huge banners went up, emblazoned with the words for "independence" and "congratulations." Another giant cake appeared on Mother Teresa Street, this time in the shape of Kosovo. Posters with U.S., European, and British flags thanked Kosovo's friends. Flags festooned Pristina; some shops contrived to make patriotic displays. One lingerie shop on Mother Teresa Street dressed its mannequins in Albanian patriotic colors—red bras, black stockings, and lacy red tops for women; black underpants for men.

On February 18, thousands of Serbs rallied in North Mitrovica, where they heard fierce speeches denouncing independence by local leaders, including by one of the most powerful, Marko Jakšić, one of the deputy heads of Koštunica's party. Serbian and Russian flags were flown and the EU denounced as an occupier. Over the previous few weeks, local Serbs had been told not to cooperate with EULEX or the ICO or rent its staff flats, houses, or offices. Over the next few days, several significant things happened. Two Kosovo UN border and customs posts to Serbia were destroyed by mobs. This, said Slobodan Samardžić, the Serbian minister for Kosovo, "might not be pleasant but it is legitimate."[4] Albanian members of the KPS no longer went north, and the structure of the police began to crack in two as Serbs said they would only take orders from UNMIK police, not from officials of the "fake" state. The de facto partition that had existed since 1999 was hardening.

In Belgrade the government announced that Serbia would treat the declaration as null and void, and charges were brought against Fatmir Sejdiu, Kosovo's president, Hashim Thaçi, and Jakup Krasniqi, the speaker of parliament, for "the declaration of a false state within Serbian borders," which was described as "a serious criminal offence against the constitution and safety of the Serbian state."[5] On February 21 the government called a massive rally in Belgrade, which gathered some 200,000 people, many of them bused in specially for the occasion. Under a huge banner reading "Kosovo is Serbia" Koštunica thundered:

What is Kosovo? Where is Kosovo? Whose is Kosovo? Is there anyone among us who is not from Kosovo? Is there anyone among us who thinks that Kosovo does not belong to us? Kosovo—that's Serbia's first name. Kosovo belongs to Serbia. Kosovo belongs to the Serbian people. That's how it has been forever. That's how it's going to be forever. There is no force, no threat, and no punishment big and hideous enough for any Serb, at any time, to say anything different but, Kosovo is Serbia![6]

The crowd then proceeded to St. Sava's church, where the Serbian Orthodox archbishop and hard-line nationalist, Metropolitan Amfilohije, said, "Kosovo and Metohija are the apple of our eye, the heart of our hearts, our holy city of Jerusalem," which he said Serbs could not renounce, either "in this worldly life nor in God's eternal one, any more than we can renounce our own soul and our own destiny."[7] A several-hundred-strong mob then attacked the U.S. embassy and set it on fire. One arsonist, a Serb who had fled from Čaglavica/Çagllavica in Kosovo in 1999, died in the fire. Other embassies were also attacked and shops looted.

In Kosovo itself, at least in the months after independence, it was unclear who was supposed to be doing what. Resolution 1244 remained in place and UNMIK was still operating, but Pieter Feith had arrived to head the ICO, wearing his hat as EU Special Representative. One of the first things he had to announce was that the EU staff would not work in the north for the time being, given the question of security. By late July neither the ICO nor EULEX were fully operational.

In the Serbian enclaves, people were nervous but they continued to exist as islands. There was no exodus, which was what many had long feared. Many Serbs still working in offices connected to the new state left their jobs or were harassed and intimidated to leave by Serbian officials and fellow Serbs. On March 14, Serbian protestors seized the court in North Mitrovica. Three days later, UN police and KFOR took it back. In the ensuing violence one Ukrainian policeman died. UNMIK accused the Serbian authorities of orchestrating the affair and said that they had proof that police from Serbia had been in the court.

Given this developing situation, one diplomat said that while the Serbs had in the past said that Kosovo's independence would result in two Albanian states in the Balkans, for now it seemed as if, by contrast, there would now be two Kosovos, a Serbian and an Albanian one. How this will work out in the long run remains to be seen, as Serb leaders had said that while they would not work with EULEX and the ICO (a position they in turn hoped and assumed would soften would over time), they would continue to work with KFOR and UNMIK, the latter of which, however, it had been assumed, would be phased out. In the wake of independence though, and given that there was no agreement on its future in the Security Council, it continued to exist.

In principle, had Kosovo's independence been achieved in a clear and universally accepted manner, ordinary Kosovars could have hoped that their leaders, who had spent so long talking about status and independence, should now look toward the real needs of their people, especially in terms of creating jobs. However, the lack of clarity of the situation meant that even with many countries recognizing Kosovo— though far fewer than they had hoped—this might yet be an optimistic scenario. Five months after the declaration, only 43 countries had formally recognized, including only 20 out of 27 EU states.[8]

Foreign investment, already scarce on the ground because of the unclear legal situation, might, it seemed, continue to be discouraged. This was bad news for a weak economy, especially as it had always been hoped that independence would help to open up new state and correct some of its worst imbalances. According to Shpend Ahmeti, director of Kosovo's Institute for Advanced Studies, imports were running at about €1.3 billion a year, but exports at a microscopic €90–130 million.

Most of Kosovo's 25,000 to 30,000 young people who came on to the labor market every year were unskilled, and educational reform was a priority. To address this need, energetic young leaders such as Enver Hoxhaj, the minister of education, were determined that now was the time for change. But he had a ministry of only 200 people, and some 500,000 students in education from primary level to university, most of whom were bursting out their buildings because so few had been built for the last 20 years. He also complained that he had 27,000 teachers, but that there was no central register to tell him if they were qualified or not.

In all sectors, from the culture of intimidation that hampered the pursuit of justice in Kosovo's clogged-up, inefficient, and often corrupt courts, to the fact that Kosovo suffered from daily power cuts—a new power station needed to be built—there was much to do, but not enough money or skilled people to do it. And yet, there were also many hopeful signs. Ahmeti noted that detailed recent surveys had shown that far from being depleted by centuries of mining, Kosovo remained rich in terms of valuable minerals and also sat on huge amounts of lignite, a form of low-quality coal. Small modern factories also existed in Kosovo, but few knew anything about them because they did not make for sexy news copy. They included food processing plants, vineyards, and other, mainly family-dominated concerns.

Two points here. One was that independence as such would not make so much difference to these businesses. Ahmet Kuçi, the commercial director of a small shoe factory called "Solid," said that his main problem was that taxes and interest rates in Kosovo were far higher than in the rest of the region and thus it was hard to compete. What would make a difference, then, would be a government concerned to nurture business and cut taxes. Kushtrim Xhakli, a young Internet entrepreneur, said Kosovo Albanians also had to think bigger than they had in the past. Business, he said, was impeded by a problem of conservative thinking and there was no tradition or experience of growing private companies larger than any one family could control. He had been trying to suggest websites for supermarkets that would enable family members abroad to pay for goods delivered in Kosovo. So far he had had no luck. "They are frightened of modern technology and losing control," he said.

The new Kosovo clearly faced huge challenges, but then so did the rest of the region. On March 8 Serbia's government collapsed. Kostunica argued that Serbia could only continue on the path to European integration if the EU states that had recognized Kosovo now rescinded their recognitions, while President Tadić argued that the best way to fight Kosovo's acceptance as a state was to continue along the road to Brussels. One of the biggest tests, however, was for the EU and its ability to use its transformative power in Kosovo and in the region as a whole.

If the situation on the ground in Kosovo, in terms of who was in charge, was unclear, the same was true internationally. The United States and most EU states recognized Kosovo, as had many other countries, but Russia, China, Brazil, India, and many others had not. Likewise, few Muslim countries recognized Kosovo, at least initially, which was a surprise given that most of its people are Muslims. Possibly the Albanians were viewed with suspicion in much of the Islamic world as, apart from being overwhelmingly secular, they are also ferociously pro-American, and in Kosovo especially there remains an enormous well of gratitude to the United States for having taken the lead in ending Serbian rule.

So, in the wake of the declaration, Kosovo began a new chapter of international uncertainty burdened with the problems of both a Taiwan, with an ambiguous international status, and a divided Cyprus. Still it was clear that a chapter had closed, even if Kosovo did not appear yet to be really, completely independent, in the sense of its people and their elected leaders being as much in charge of their own destinies as is possible in the modern world. Even if this was not immediately clear to most Kosovo Albanians after the declaration of independence, some, at least, had no illusions. Ylber Hysa, a former student activist, journalist, deputy, and now an analyst working at Pristina's Institute for Albanian Studies, said that as far as he was concerned the important thing was not so much independence as "Serbia out."

NOTES

Chapter 1

1. Statistics from tables of Census Data, 1948–1991, taken from Julie Mertus, *Kosovo: How Myths and Truths Started a War* (Berkeley: University of California Press, 1999). Also in Tim Judah, *Kosovo: War and Revenge* (New Haven: Yale University Press, 2002). Original source: *Jugoslavija 1918–1988, statistički godišnjak Jugoslavije za 1992, godinu* (1992), pp. 62–63, as cited in Milan Vučković and Goran Nikolić, *Stanovništvo Kosova u razdoblju od 1918 do 1991 godine* (Munich, 1996), pp. 108–109. Statistics are also now reproduced by the Statistical Office of Kosovo; however, Montenegrins are listed as "others" by them. See note 5 below.

2. Statistical Office of Kosovo, *Kosovo and Its Population*, September 2003. Available here: http://www.ks-gov.net/ESK/esk/pdf/english/population/Kosovo_population.pdf.

3. Statistical Office of Kosovo, *Demographic Changes of the Kosovo Population, 1948–2006* (Pristina, February 2008). Statistics, p. 23; quote, p. 24. Available here: http://www.ks-gov.net/ESK/esk/pdf/english/population/Demographic%20changes%20of%20the%20Kosovo%20population%201948–2006.pdf.

4. http://www.ks-gov.net/ESK/esk/english/english.htm.

5. European Stability Initiative, *Cutting the Lifeline: Migration, Families and the Future of Kosovo* (Berlin and Istanbul, 2006), p. 7. The

report includes a history and analysis of Kosovo Albanian migration for work. Available here: http://www.esiweb.org/pdf/esi_document_id_80.pdf.

6. For a discussion of this and the broader issues of Macedonian Albanians, see Nadège Ragaru, "The Former Yugoslav Republic of Macedonia: Between Ohrid and Brussels," in Judy Batt, ed., *Is There an Albanian Question?* European Union, Institute for Security Studies, Chaillot Paper 107 (Paris, January 2008).

7. Republic of Macedonia, State Statistical Office. "Census of Population, Households and Dwellings in the Republic of Macedonia, 2002." Available here: http://www.stat.gov.mk/pdf/kniga_13.pdf.

8. Republic of Serbia, Statistical Office, Communication No. 295, Issue Lll, December 24, 2002, "Final Results of the Census, 2002." Available here: http://www.statserb.sr.gov.yu/zip/esn31.pdf.

9. For Montenegrin statistics, see http://www.monstat.cg.yu/EngPrva.htm.

10. Republic of Albania, Institute of Statistics, *Albania in Figures* (Tirana, 2005).

11. For a concise summary of the Çamëria story and one which brings it up to date, see Miranda Vickers, *The Cham Issue: Albanian National & Property Claims in Greece*. Conflict Studies Research Centre, April 2002, G109. The center has since been renamed the Advanced Research and Assessment Group and is part of Britain's Defence Academy. It has done a lot of valuable work on the Balkans, which is freely available. See http://www.da.mod.uk/colleges/csrc.

12. A variation on his name is Vaso Pasho or Pasha.

13. "Fatos Lubonja. Between the Glory of a Virtual World and the Misery of a Real World," in *Albanian Identities: Myth and History*, edited by Stephanie Schwandner-Sievers and Bernd J. Fischer (London: Hurst, 2002), p. 91. The word *bajrak* means banner. The *bajraktar* was a local boss entrusted with raising men in time of conflict.

Chapter 2

1. The so-called Republic of Serbian Krajina lasted from 1991 until 1995.

2. For Serbia, see Republic of Serbia, Statistical Office, Communication No. 295, Issue Lll, 24 December 2002, "Final Results of the Census, 2002," available here: http://www.statserb.sr.gov.yu/zip/esn31.pdf. Like Kosovo, no census has been conducted in Bosnia since 1991. See United Nations High Commissioner for Refugees (UNHCR), http://www.unhcr.ba/index.htm; Agency for Statistics for Bosnia and Herzegovina, http://www.bhas.ba/eng/BiHStats.asp?Pripadnost=4&mode=dark; and Republika Srpska Institute of Statistics, http://www.rzs.rs.ba/PublikDemENG.htm. For Croatia, see Central Bureau of Statistics, http://www.dzs.hr/default_e.htm. For Montenegro, see http://www.monstat.cg.yu/EngPrva.htm. For Macedonia, see State Statistical Office, "Census of Population, Household and Dwellings in the Republic of Macedonia, 2002," available here: http://www.stat.gov.mk/pdf/kniga_13.pdf.

3. Božidar Djelić, *Serbia: Things Will Get Better* (Belgrade, 2007), pp. 252–255.

Chapter 3

1. Anne Pennington and Peter Levi, *Marko the Prince: Serbo-Croat Heroic Songs* (London: Duckworth, 1984), pp. 17–18.

2. Thomas Emmert, *Serbian Golgotha: Kosovo 1389* (New York: Columbia University Press, 1990), p. 129.

3. Jean-Arnault Dérens, *Le Piège du Kosovo* (Paris: Editions Non Lieu, 2008), p. 46.

4. Ibid., pp. 227–228.

5. Lenard Cohen, *Serpent in the Bosom: The Rise and Fall of Slobodan Milošević* (Boulder, Colo.: Westview Press, 2001), p. 4.

6. Fatos Lubonja, "Between the Glory of a Virtual World and the Misery of a Real World," in *Albanian Identities: Myth and History,*

edited by Stephanie Schwandner-Sievers and Bernd J. Fischer (London: Hurst, 2002), p. 92.

7. Ibid., p. 93.

8. The Arbëresh are the Albanian Christian minority of southern Italy.

9. Piro Misha, "Invention of a Nationalism: Myth and Amnesia," in Fischer and Schwandner-Sievers, *Albanian Identities*, p. 43.

10. Anna Di Lellio and Stephanie Schwandner-Sievers, "The Legendary Commander: The Construction of an Albanian Master-narrative in Post-war Kosovo," *Nations and Nationalism* 12.3 (2006): 518.

11. Anna Di Lellio and Stephanie Schwandner-Sievers, "Sacred Journey to a Nation: The Construction of a Shrine in Postwar Kosovo," *Journeys* 7.1 (June 2006): 29.

12. Fatos Bytyci, *Blood Feuds Revive in Unstable Kosovo*. BCR No. 481, February 19, 2004. Institute for War and Peace Reporting.

Chapter 4

1. Noel Malcolm, *Kosovo: A Short History* (London: Macmillan, 1998). On this, see chapter 8, "The Austrian Invasion and the 'Great Migration' of the Serbs: 1689–1690."

2. Thomas Emmert, *Serbian Golgotha: Kosovo 1389* (New York: Columbia University Press, 1990), p. 133.

3. Carnegie Endowment for International Peace, *Report of the International Commission to Inquire into the Causes and Conduct of the Balkan Wars* (Washington, D.C., 1914), p. 151. Republished in 1993 under the title *The Other Balkan Wars*.

4. Andrej Mitrović, *Serbia's Great War, 1914–1918* (London: Hurst, 2007), p. 159.

5. Jean-Arnault Dérens, *Le Piège du Kosovo* (Paris: Editions Non Lieu, 2008), p. 60.

Chapter 5

1. Noel Malcolm, *Kosovo: A Short History* (London: Macmillan, 1998), p. 273.

2. Denisa Kostovicova, "Shkolla Shqipe" and "Nationhood," in *Albanian Identities: Myth and History*, edited by Stephanie Schwandner-Sievers and Bernd J. Fischer (London: Hurst, 2002), p. 159.

3. Ibid., p. 162.

4. Jean-Arnault Dérens, *Le Piège du Kosovo* (Paris: Editions Non Lieu, 2008), p. 64. I am grateful for several details here.

5. Ibid., p. 65.

6. Ibrahim Berisha et al., eds., *Serbian Colonization and Ethnic Cleansing of Kosova: Documents & Evidence* (Pristina, 1993), pp. 21–23.

7. Bernd J. Fischer, *Albania at War, 1939–1945* (London: Hurst, 1999), p. 86.

8. Ibid., p. 180.

9. Ibid., p. 87.

10. Ibid., p. 185.

11. Malcolm, *Kosovo*, p. 308.

12. Ibid., p. 315.

13. Miranda Vickers, *The Albanians: A Modern History* (London: I. B. Tauris, 1995), p. 165, citing *Zëri I Popullit*, May 17, 1981.

14. Dérens, *Le Piège du Kosovo*, p. 71.

Chapter 6

1. Miranda Vickers, *Between Serb and Albanian: A History of Kosovo* (London: Hurst, 1998), p. 152.

2. Ibid., p. 187.

3. See the picture story about this on the website of the European Stability Initiative (ESI), *A Future for Pristina's Past* (March 2006), at http://www.esiweb.org/index.php?lang=en&id=281&story_ID=12.

4. This is part of a profile I wrote of Migjen Kelmendi for the European Stability Initiative. The full interview is here: http://www.esiweb.org/index.php?lang=en&id=280&portrait_ID=7.

5. Statistics from tables of census data 1948–1991 taken from Julie Mertus, *Kosovo: How Myths and Truths Started a War* (Berkeley: University of California Press, 1999). Also in Tim Judah, *Kosovo: War and Revenge* (New Haven: Yale University Press, 2002). Original source: *Jugoslavija 1918–1988*. Statistics are also now reproduced by the Statistical Office of Kosovo; however, Montenegrins are listed as "others" by them.

6. This is part of a profile I wrote of Branislav Krstić for the European Stability Initiative. The full interview is here: http://www.esiweb .org/index.php?lang=en&id=280&portrait_ID=1.

7. Kosta Mihailović and Vasilije Krestić, *Memorandum of the Serbian Academy of Sciences and Arts: Answers to Criticisms* (Belgrade, 1995). The various quotations from the Memorandum here appear on pp. 119–140.

Chapter 7

1. An earlier notorious incident was that of the Kosovo Serb farmer Djordje Martinović, who in May 1985 alleged he had been attacked by two Albanians who had left a bottle pushed up his rear. The local authorities claimed it was self-inflicted while Serbian academics claimed that this reminded them of the Ottoman practice of impaling victims on stakes.

2. Laura Silber and Allan Little, *The Death of Yugoslavia* (London: Penguin, 1995), p. 66.

3. Ibid., p. 77.

4. Miranda Vickers, *Between Serb and Albanian: A History of Kosovo* (London: Hurst, 1998), p. 264, quoting Rugova from *Impact International*, April 10–May 7, 1992, p. 10.

5. Barton Gellman, "How the US and Allies Went to War," *Washington Post*, April 18, 1999.

6. Denisa Kostovicova, *Parallel Worlds: Response of Kosovo Albanians to Loss of Autonomy in Serbia, 1989–1996* (Keele, U.K.: Keele University Press, 1997), pp. 33–35.

7. International Crisis Group (ICG), *Kosovo Spring* (Pristina and Sarajevo, 1998), p. 21; and Denisa Kostovicova, "Albanian Schooling in Kosovo: 1992–1998: 'Liberty Imprisoned,'" in *Kosovo: Myths, Conflict and War*, edited by Kyril Drezov, Bulent Gokay, and Denisa Kostovicova (Keele, U.K.: Keele University Press, 1999), p. 15.

8. This is part of a profile I wrote of Rona Nishliu for the European Stability Initiative. The full interview is here: http://www.esiweb .org/index.php?lang=en&id=280&portrait_ID=8.

Chapter 8

1. Haradinaj was acquitted on April 3, 2008. He was feted on his return. The presiding judge, Alphonsus Orie, said, "The Chamber gained a strong impression that the trial was being held in an atmosphere where witnesses felt unsafe." See press release: "Haradinaj and Balaj acquitted of all charges, Brahimaj guilty of cruel treatment and torture in Jablanica compound," The Hague, April 3, 2008. NJ/MOW/1232e. See http://www.un.org/icty/pressreal/2008/pr1232e.htm.

2. Bardh Hamzaj, *A Narrative about War and Freedom. Dialog with the Commander Ramush Haradinaj* (Pristina: Zeri, 2000), p. 31.

3. Ibid., p. 32.

4. Madeleine Albright, *Madam Secretary: A Memoir* (New York: Miramax, 2003), p. 386.

5. Hamzaj, *Narrative*, p. 115.

6. Marc Weller, "Interim Agreement," in *The Crisis in Kosovo 1989–1999: From the Dissolution of Yugoslavia to Rambouillet and the Outbreak of Hostilities* (Cambridge, 1999), p. 469.

7. Albright, *Madam Secretary*, p. 403.

8. United Nations High Commissioner for Refugees (UNHCR), *Refugees*, vol. 3, no. 116, 1999, p. 11.

9. David Gowan, "Kosovo's Moment, Serbia's Chance," *Survival* 50.2 (April–May 2008): 6.

10. Human Rights Watch, *Under Orders: War Crimes in Kosovo* (New York: Human Rights Watch, 2001), p. 16.

11. Gowan, "Kosovo's Moment, Serbia's Chance." I am grateful to Gezim Rezha of the OSCE for the Meja figures. He survived the selection process of men to be killed, taken off the convoy of vehicles passing through Meja by the police. As of March 2008, 345 bodies had been returned, identified, and buried. There were still 32 missing. The dead were both Muslims and Catholics but they were buried together. According to Rezha: "The remains were not returned all at once, but in groups and at different periods in time, starting in May 2003. Their return in groups caused more pain and suffering to the families, keeping them in a constant state of anxiety and grief. From 1999–2003 the relatives of the missing people did their best to try and find them, hoping that they were still alive, perhaps, somewhere in the prisons of Serbia."

12. OSCE, *Kosovo/Kosova: As Seen, As Told. Part II. A Report on the Human Rights Findings of the OSCE Mission in Kosovo. June to October 1999* (Pristina, 1999), pp. 122–123.

Chapter 9

1. United Nations Security Council, Resolution 1244 (1999).

2. UNMIK, Fact Sheet, *Kosovo in February 2008*.

3. See Misha Glenny, "Balkan Organized Crime," in *Is There an Albanian Question?* edited by Judy Batt, EU Institute for Security Studies, Chaillot Paper 107 (Paris, 2008). This chapter is based on part of his book *McMafia: Crime without Frontiers* (London: Bodley Head, 2008).

4. UNMIK, Fact Sheet, *Kosovo in February 2008*.

5. Serbian Government, "Internally Displaced Persons and Expellees from Kosovo and Metohija." See http://www.srbija.sr.gov.yu/kosovo-metohija/?id=8929.

6. Some 16,000 of this number may have been Serb refugees from Croatia and Bosnia, although technically they would have been

"refugees" coming from what were now different states, rather than "internally displaced people" (IDPs), which is the technical jargon for refugees within their own country. See also Tim Judah, *Kosovo: War and Revenge* (New Haven: Yale University Press, 2002), p. 130, which covers KLA attacks against these refugees.

7. European Stability Initiative, *The Lausanne Principal. Multiethnicity, Territory and the Future of Kosovo's Serbs* (Berlin and Pristina, 2004), p. 2.

8. Serbian Government, "Former Employees in Kosovo Institutions to Get Jobs in Serbian State Organs," April 2, 2008. See http://www.srbija.sr.gov.yu/vesti/vest.php?id=44742.

9. UNMIK, Fact Sheet, *Kosovo in February 2008*.

10. Iniciativa Kosovare për Stabilitet/Kosovar Stability Initiative (IKS), *Getting to Lisbon: Accessing Vocational Training Needs and Job Creation Opportunities for Rural Women* (Prishtina, April 2008), p. 14.

11. Ibid., pp. 17–18.

12. Ibid., p. 15.

Chapter 10

1. UNMIK, "Standards for Kosovo." See http://www.unmikonline.org/standards/index.html.

2. Ibid. See http://www.unmikonline.org/standards/docs/leaflet_stand_eng.pdf.

3. The issue of missing people has dogged Kosovo since the end of the war. Thus it is worth quoting in full this, from UNMIK's February 2008 Fact Sheet: "A total of 5,206 people were reported missing in Kosovo after the conflict in 1998–99. By the end of 2007, 1,998 persons (Kosovo Albanians, Kosovo Serbs and other ethnic minorities) where still listed as missing according to International Committee of the Red Cross (ICRC) figures. Between 2002 and December 2007, the Office on Missing Persons and Forensics (OMPF) reduced the number of missing persons by over 50 percent. As of end December 2007, 1,950 missing persons have

been pronounced dead and have had their remains returned to their families. In addition, 100 missing persons have been identified, but the families have chosen not to accept the bodies until other members of their families or communities are found so they can be buried together. As of December 2007, there are around 455 individuals whose remains have not yet been identified."

4. For a detailed report on the March events, see Human Rights Watch, *Failure to Protect: Anti-Minority Violence in Kosovo, March 2004.* 16.6 (D) (July 2004).

5. UN Security Council S/2005/635, letter dated October 7, 2005, from the secretary general addressed to the president of the Security Council. Annex: *A Comprehensive Review of the Situation in Kosovo.* See http://www.unosek.org/docref/KaiEidereport.pdf.

6. UN Security Council, letter dated March 26, 2007, from the secretary general addressed to the president of the Security Council, S/2007/168, p. 2. This constitutes the covering report of Ahtisaari to the UN, which accompanied his plan. The official name of the plan is the Comprehensive Proposal for the Kosovo Status Settlement. Both the report and plan can be found at http://www.unosek .org/unosek/en/statusproposal.html.

7. European Union, "Preparing for a Future International and EU Presence in Kosovo." You can see the leaflet at http://www.eupt-kosovo .eu/new/home/docs/EU_booklet%20ENG_Jan%202008.pdf.

8. UN Security Council, letter dated March 26, 2007, p. 8, covering the report of the Ahtisaari plan.

9. Kosovo's declaration of independence can be found on the website of Kosovo's Assembly: http://www.assembly-kosova.org/?krye= news&newsid=1635&lang=en.

Chapter 11

1. UNDP: Early Warning Report, Kosovo, *Report #11. July–September 2005,* p. 34.

2. Migjen Kelmendi, "Arbën Xhaferi's Ethnic Albania or Teuta Arifi's Political Nation?" in Migjen Kelmendi and Arlinda Desku, *Who Is Kosovar? Kosovar Identity: A Debate* (Pristina, 2005), p. 101.

3. See World Bank, Kosovo Monthly Economic Briefing, April 2006. Available here: http://web.worldbank.org/WBSITE/EXTERNAL/COUNTRIES/ECAEXT/KOSOVOEXTN/0,,contentMDK:20953280~menuPK:1604547~pagePK:1497618~piPK:217854~theSitePK:297770,00.html.

4. *Albania Quarterly*, World Bank Country Office Newsletter, No. 5, March 2006. Available here: http://siteresources.worldbank.org/INTALBANIA/News%20and%20Events/20869874/newsletter5.pdf.

5. *The Economist*, podcast, *Veton Surroi on Kosovo*, "Certain Ideas of Europe," March 14, 2008; http://audiovideo.economist.com/?fr_story=a65531e1f05c29947b4b8949d786de25f7e1fa9d&rf=bm.

6. "Existence of Bosnia and Herzegovina Cannot Be Questioned," Office of the High Representative and EU Special Representative (OHR) press release, January 30, 2008.

7. Thanos Veremis, "The Chances of Post-Modernity in the Balkans," paper delivered at the European Council on Foreign Relations, Sofia, November 19, 2007.

Chapter 12

1. Pavel Felgenhauer, "The Tactics and Strategic Goals of Russia's Stand on the Independence of Kosovo," Real Instituto Elcano, Madrid. ARI 125/2007. 30/11/2007. See http://www.realinstitutoelcano.org/wps/portal/rielcano_eng/Content?WCM_GLOBAL_CONTEXT=/Elcano_in/Zonas_in/ARI125-2007.

2. "Russia: Putin Calls for 'Universal Principles' to Settle Frozen Conflict," Radio Free Europe/Radio Liberty (RFE/RL), February 1, 2006.

3. Victor Yasmann, "Moscow Content to Block Kosovo Resolution," RFE/RL, July 13, 2007.

4. Evelyn Leopold, "Russia Rejects West's UN Plan on Kosovo's Future," Reuters, July 17, 2007.

5. Yasmann, "Moscow Content."

6. Ibid.

7. Brian Whitmore, "Russia: Moscow Turns Its Attention to the Balkans," RFE/RL, June 27, 2007.

8. Daniel Fried, U.S. Assistant Secretary of State for European and Eurasian Affairs, "Remarks before the U.S. Senate Foreign Relations Committee," Washington, D.C., June 21, 2007. http://www .state.gov/p/eur/rls/rm/86990.htm.

9. Mark Leonard and Nicu Popescu, *A Power Audit of EU-Russia Relations*, ECFR (London, 2007), p. 2. http://www.ecfr.eu/content/entry/ eu_russia_relations.

Chapter 13

1. Kosovo's new flag was not seen in public before the declaration. There had been a public contest to design the banner, but it was unclear how exactly the final choice was made. According to one diplomatic source, a committee had decided on a flag with 12 stars but that they had been told from Brussels that it was unacceptable because the European flag has 12 stars. So they chopped the number in half. When the flag appeared, people were told that the six stars represented six ethnic communities, but some believed that in fact they represented the six regions of Albanian settlement, namely, Kosovo, Albania, Macedonia, Montenegro, Çamëria, and Preševo/Presheva.

2. Kosovo's declaration of independence can be found on the website of Kosovo's Assembly: http://www.assembly-kosova.org/?krye= news&newsid=1635&lang=en.

3. Ibid.

4. "Minister Samardzic: Setting Fire to the Border Crossings Is Legitimate," VIP Daily News Report, Belgrade, February 20, 2008 (No. 3785).

5. "MUP Files Criminal Charges against Thaci, Sejdiu and Krasniqi," VIP Daily News Report, Belgrade, February 19, 2008 (No. 3784).

6. Vojislav Kostunica, "Serbia Has and Will Annul Every Act of the Fictitious State on its Territory," February 21, 2008. Serbian Government website: http://www.srbija.sr.gov.yu/vesti/vest .php?id=43419&q.

7. Sermon of Metropolitan Amfilohije, February 21, 2008. See http:// www.orthodoxengland.org.uk/sermmetam.htm.

8. This site keeps a tally: http://www.kosovothanksyou.com.

BIBLIOGRAPHY

This is a limited bibliography. Many more books have been written about Kosovo, or discuss Kosovo in one relevant way or another. These are books that have either been used while writing this book or would make for useful further reading and are mostly relatively up to date and easily accessible. With a few French exceptions, these are all books in English.

Albright, Madeleine. *Madam Secretary: A Memoir.* New York: Miramax, 2003.

Banac, Ivo. *The National Question in Yugoslavia. Origins, History, Politics.* Ithaca, N.Y.: Cornell University Press, 1984.

Batt, Judy, ed. *Is There an Albanian Question?* European Union, Institute for Security Studies, Chaillot Paper 107. Paris, 2008.

Buckley, William Joseph. *Kosovo: Contending Voices on Balkan Interventions.* Grand Rapids, Mich.: William B. Eerdmans, 2000.

Caplan, Richard. *Europe and the Recognition of New States in Yugoslavia.* Cambridge: Cambridge University Press, 2005.

———. *International Governance of War-Torn Territories: Rule and Reconstruction.* New York: Oxford University Press, 2005.

Cohen, Lenard J. *Serpent in the Bosom: The Rise and Fall of Slobodan Milošević.* Boulder, Colo.: Westview Press, 2001.

Deimel, Johanna, and Wim van Meurs. *The Balkan Prism: A Retrospective by Policy-Makers and Analysts*. Munich: Otto Sagner, 2007.

Dérens, Jean-Arnault. *Balkans: La crise*. Paris: Gallimard, 2000.

——. *Le Piège du Kosovo*. Paris: Editions Non Lieu, 2008.

Dérens, Jean-Arnault, and Laurent Geslin. *Comprendre les Balkans: Histoire, sociétés, perspectives*. Paris: Editions Non Lieu, 2007.

Di Lellio, Anna. *The Case for Kosova: Passage to Independence*. New York: Anthem Press, 2006.

Durham, Edith. *High Albania*. London: Phoenix, 2000. First published in 1909 by E. Arnold.

——. *Albania and the Albanians. Selected Articles and Letters 1903–1944*. London: Centre for Albanian Studies, 2001.

Fischer, Bernd J. *Albania at War, 1939–1945*. London: Hurst, 1999.

——, ed. *Balkan Strongmen: Dictators and Authoritarian Rulers of Southeast Europe*. London: Hurst, 2006.

Hamzaj, Bardh. *A Narrative about War and Freedom. Dialog with Commander Ramush Haradinaj*. Pristina: Zeri, 2000.

Hockenos, Paul. *Homeland Calling: Exile Patriotism and the Balkan Wars*. Ithaca, N.Y.: Cornell University Press, 2003.

Hodgkinson, Harry. *Scanderbeg*. Edited by Bejtullah Destani and Westrow Cooper. London: Centre for Albanian Studies, 1999.

Human Rights Watch. *Under Orders: War Crimes in Kosovo*. New York: Human Rights Watch, 2001.

Independent International Commission on Kosovo. *The Kosovo Report: Conflict, International Response, Lessons Learned*. Oxford: Oxford University Press, 2000.

Judah, Tim. *Kosovo: War and Revenge*. New Haven: Yale University Press, 2002.

——. *The Serbs: History, Myth and the Destruction of Yugoslavia*. New Haven: Yale University Press, 2000.

Kelmendi, Migjen, and Arlinda Desku. *Who Is Kosovar? Kosovar Identity: A Debate*. Pristina, 2005.

King, Iain, and Whit Mason. *Peace at Any Price: How the World Failed Kosovo*. London: Hurst, 2006.

Kola, Paulin. *The Search for Greater Albania*. London: Hurst, 2003.

Kouchner, Bernard. *Les Guerriers de la paix. Du Kosovo à l'Irak*. Paris: Grasset, 2004.

Krstić-Brano, Branislav. *Kosovo: Facing the Court of History*. Amherst, N.Y.: Humanity, 2004.

LeBor, Adam. *Milosevic: A Biography*. London: Bloomsbury, 2002.

Malcolm, Noel. *Kosovo: A Short History*. London: Macmillan, 1998.

Mertus, Julie A. *Kosovo: How Myths and Truths Started a War*. Berkeley: University of California Press, 1999.

Mitrović, Andrej. *Serbia's Great War, 1914–1918*. London: Hurst, 2007.

OSCE (Organization for Security and Cooperation in Europe). *Kosovo/ Kosova: As Seen, As Told. Part II. A Report on the Human Rights Findings of the OSCE Mission in Kosovo. June to October 1999*. Pristina, 1999.

OSCE/ODIHR (Organization for Security and Cooperation in Europe/ Office for Democratic Institutions and Human Rights). *Kosovo/ Kosova: As Seen, As Told—An Analysis of the Human Rights findings of the OSCE Kosovo Verification Mission, October 1998 to June 1999*. Warsaw, 1999.

Pavlowitch, Stevan K. *Serbia: The History behind the Name*. London: Hurst, 2002.

——. *Hitler's New Disorder: The Second World War in Yugoslavia*. London: Hurst, 2008.

Pettifer, James. *Kosova Express: A Journey in Wartime*. London: Hurst, 2005.

Pettifer, James, and Miranda Vickers. *The Albanian Question: Reshaping the Balkans*. London: I. B. Tauris, 2007.

Schwandner-Sievers, Stephanie, and Bernd J. Fischer, eds. *Albanian Identities: Myth and History*. London: Hurst, 2002.

Sell, Louis. *Slobodan Milosevic and the Destruction of Yugoslavia*. Durham, N.C.: Duke University Press, 2002.

Surroi, Veton. *Azem Berisha's One and Only Flight to the Castle*. Prishtina, 2005.

Vickers, Miranda. *Between Serb and Albanian: A History of Kosovo*. London: Hurst, 1998.

Warrander, Gail, and Verena Knaus. *Kosovo. The Bradt Travel Guide*. Chalfont St. Peter, U.K.: Bradt, 2007.

Websites

Google Kosovo and you will find a number of sites dealing with it, either from a Serbian or an Albanian point of view. You will also find relevant sites for UNMIK, EULEX, the ICO, and Serbian and Kosovo institutions. Three sites deserve particular mention here. They cover the whole of the Balkans including Kosovo, and their coverage is consistently excellent and unbiased. For daily news and analysis see Balkan Insight (balkaninsight.com). For more in-depth and analytical coverage, see the European Stability Initiative (esiweb.org). If you read French, turn to Le Courier des Balkans (balkans.courriers.info).

INDEX

Abkhazia, 128, 132–33
Aceh, xviii
aerial bombardment, 46, 68, 75, 87–88, 90,
    108, 137
    civilian deaths from, 89
Afghanistan, xv
Agani, Fehmi, 72, 85
Ahmeti, Ali, 121
Ahmeti, Shpend, 148, 149
Ahtisaari, Martti, 90, 108, 111, 113–14, 136
Ahtisaari plan, 108, 111, 113–16, 136–37,
    139
    implementation agreement, 142, 145
Alamo, battle of the (1836), 27–28
Albania, xv
    Albanian resident population
        estimate for, 6–7
    collapse into anarchy (1997) of, 80
    communism and, 8, 25, 47, 49, 76
    demilitarized zone and, 43
    flag of, 27, 98, 144
    independence (1912) of, 10, 38, 118
    Kosovo Albanian refugees in, 88
    Kosovo war and, 75, 80–81, 84–85, 92
    Kosovo's relationship with, 75, 92,
        119–23, 125, 138
    Montenegrin Army in, 38
    national day (November 28) of, 38, 81
    nationalism and, 9–11, 26–27, 35, 36,
        44, 77, 119, 120–21
    Ottoman control of, 7, 9–10, 19, 25,
        34–35, 36, 37, 39, 44, 117, 120
    political parties in, 121
    religious identity and, 8–9, 44
    Serbian Army in, 38
    square mileage of, 127
    standard literary language of, 118
    Turks and education policy 44
    World War I and, 40

    World War II and, 46–47, 48
    Young Turks and, 37, 39
    Zog's leadership and, 43, 47, 48
    See also Greater Albania; Kosovo
        Albanians
Albanian language, 15, 17, 101, 104
    Gheg dialect, 9, 120
    as shared identity, 9
    standard literary, 118
    Tosk dialect, 9, 118
    university studies in, 53
Albanians, 1–11
    in Albania, 6–7
    blood feuds and, 28–29
    collaborationist charges against, 7, 52
    diasporas abroad of, 3, 6, 7, 11, 52, 73,
        74, 77, 118
    emigration to Turkey, 46, 52
    Greater Albania concept and, 120–21
    in Greece, 6, 7, 120
    in Italy, 6, 7
    key characteristics of, 7–10
    in Macedonia, 3–4, 8, 33, 42, 121–22,
        123
    in Montenegro, 5–6, 7, 52–53
    national identity and, 29, 44, 118
    religion and, 6, 7–9, 25–26, 31, 32, 33,
        34, 118
    in Serbia, 5
    Yugoslav status of, 54, 118
    See also Kosovo Albanians
Albright, Madeleine, 83, 86
Amfilohije, Metropolitan, 147
Anatolia, 46
Annan, Kofi, 110–11
Arbëresh, 7, 26
Arbour, Louise, 90
Arifi, Teuta, 122
Armenians, 132

Arsenije III, Patriarch, 33
Ashkali, 104
Austria
    Albanian diaspora in, 3, 16,
    Ottoman advance on, 33, 34
Austro-Hungarian Empire, 35, 37–41, 44
Azerbaijan, 132

Badinter, Robert, 130–31
Badinter Commission, 131
Bajrami, Agron, 143
Balkan Federation (proposed), 49
"Balkan Ghetto," xv, 128
Balkans
    Albanians and, 1, 118
    Congress of Berlin and, 23, 35, 126
    nationalism and, 35
    Ottoman collapse in, 37
    Russia and, 138
    social problems in, 98
    See also Slavs; Western Balkans;
        specific countries and ethnic groups
Balkan wars (1912, 1913), 7, 11, 15, 37–39,
    41, 42
Balkan wars (1990s), xv, xvii, 12, 13, 14,
    15, 27, 28, 41, 68–70, 121
    beginning of, 61, 68
    demilitarized zone and, 43
    international public opinion and, 83
    legacies of, 125
    Western guilt and, 68, 87
    See also Bosnian war; Croatian war;
        Kosovo war
Ban Ki-moon, 141
Barthes, Roland, 72
Basque separatists, xviii, 134, 135
Batajnica air base, 90
Bayezid, sultan, 20
Bejta, Azem, 43
Bektashism, 8
Belgrade, 5, 20, 59, 64, 89, 125
    capture of (1688), 33
    Nazi bombing of, 46
    rally against Kosovo independence
        in, 146–47
Belgrade University, 15, 46
Berisha, Sali, 80
Bitola/Monastir, 117
Black Sea, 128, 132
blood feuds, 28, 29
Boletin, Isa, 39
Bonn, 73
Bonn Powers, 116
Bosnia (later Bosnia-Hercegovina), xv, 32,
    41, 48, 69, 75, 115–16, 123–26, 131
    Austro-Hungarian occupation of,
        35, 37
    European Union peacekeeping troops
        in, 134, 135

religious identity and, 9, 17 (see also
    Bosniaks)
Republika Srpska (RS) and, 124
self-determination and, 124
Serbia and, 32–33, 69–70, 124, 125
Serb population percentage in, 13, 14
Serb refugees from, 14, 15
See also Bosnian war
Bosniaks, 17, 33, 35, 104
    ethnic cleansing and, 124
    in Kosovo, 3
    Kosovo areas of (2008), 112 (map)
    religion as defining identity of, 9
    war deaths of (1990s), 68
    Yugoslav status of, 54
Bosnian Croats, 125
Bosnian Serbs, 13, 14, 15, 62, 91, 125
Bosnian war (1992–1995), 61, 68, 69, 70, 78
    causes of, 124
    Dayton peace agreement and, 79, 82,
        87, 124
    Srebrenica massacre and, 68, 87
Bošnjačka Mahala, 143
Branković, Vuk, 20
Brazil, 150
breakaway regions. See separatist regions
Bridge Watchers, 101
Britain, 3, 40, 41, 45, 135, 145
Bujan, 48
Bujanovac/Bujanoc, 5, 52
Bukoshi, Bujar, 73, 78, 85
Bulgaria, xv, 20, 35, 36, 118, 128
    Balkan war of 1912 and 1913 and,
        37, 38
    World War I and, 40, 41
    World War II and, 47
Bush, George H. W., 71
Bush, George W., 138

Čaglavica/Çagllavica, 109, 110, 147
Çamëria, 52, 120
Canada, 16
Carnegie Endowment, 39–40
car number plates, 100, 101
Catalan separatists, 135
Catholics, 6, 7, 8, 9, 17, 27, 31, 32, 33
Çeku, Agim, 96–97
cell phone networks, 99, 101
census (1948), 51
census (1981), 1–2
census (1991), 101
census (2002), 4, 5, 13
census (2003), 5
Çetta, Anton, 28–29
CFSP (Common Foreign and Security
    Policy), 134, 135, 139
Chad, 134
Chechnya, 130, 131
Chernomyrdin, Victor, 90

Chetniks, 49, 51
China, 141, 150
"Christmas warning" (1992), 71
Churkin, Vitaly, 136, 137
Cohen, Lenard, 24
Committee for the National Defence of
    Kosovo (KK), 42
Common Foreign and Security Policy
    (CFSP), 134, 135, 139
communism, 15, 64
    Albania and, 8, 25, 47, 49, 76
    demise of, 28, 65, 119
    dissolution of former federations
        under, 130
    Kosovo and, 51, 58, 69, 75
    Serbia and, 64–65, 66
    Serbian Orthodox resistance to, 24
    Yugoslavia and, 13, 49, 51, 61, 71
concentration camps, 47
Congress of Berlin (1878), 23, 35, 126
Corfu, 41
Corsica, 28
Ćosić, Dobrica, 61, 62
crime, 98, 114, 128, 135
Croatia, 13, 32
    Bosnia and, 125
    European Union and, 130
    expulsion of ethnic minorities
        from, 52
    golden age (1970s) in, 55
    independence declaration (1991)
        by, 68
    nationalism and, 67
    self-determination and, 131
    Serbian charges against, 66
    Serbian expansion into, 69
    Serb population in, 13, 14, 33, 62, 63
    as Yugoslav republic, 41, 53, 105
Croatian war (1991), 61, 68, 70, 78, 79, 83
Croats, xv, 15, 70, 104, 120
    in Bosnia, 125
    Greater Croatia and, 119
    religion-defined identity of, 9, 17, 32
Crockett, Davy, 28
Čubrilović, Vaso, 46
currency, xv, 98, 101, 105
Curri, Bajram, 43
Cyprus, 135, 139, 151
Cyrillic alphabet, 98, 100
Czechoslovakia, dissolution of, xvii, 130

Dalmatia, 32, 41
Dardania, 18, 31
Darfur, 134
Dayton peace agreement (1995), 79, 82,
    87, 124
Debar, 4, 121
Dečani/Deçan, 38
    church of, 19, 30

declaration of independence (Kosovo),
    text of, xiii, xvii, 144–45
Del Ponte, Carla, 92
Demaçi, Adem, 76, 86
democracy, 97, 109
Democratic League of Kosovo (LDK)
    founding of, 69
    nonviolence and, 70–71, 72, 78, 79
    post–Kosovo war and, 96
Dérens, Jean-Arnault, 23, 24, 52
diasporas, Albanian, 3, 6, 7, 11, 45–46, 73,
    74, 77, 118
Di Lellio, Anna, 27
dinar, 98
diplomacy, 82, 83–87, 130
    recognition of Bosnia and, 124
    recognition of Kosovo and, xvii, 135,
        139, 148, 150
    See also international community
displaced persons. See refugees
Djakovica/Gjakova, 30, 38, 60–61
    fires in/Kosovo Albanian
        deportations from, 88
Djelić, Božidar, 16
Dodik, Milorad, 124
Dolce Vita Café (Mitrovica), 101
"Downfall of the Serbian Empire, The"
    (epic poem), 21–23
Dragaš/Dragash, 104
Drenica region, 43, 49, 81
    war refugees from, 87
Dubrovnik, 20
    siege of (1991), 68
Dukagjini, Lek, 28, 29
Dukagjin plateau, 30
Dušan, Tsar ("Emperor of the Serbs and
    Greeks"), 19–20
Dzittsojty, Juri, 133

"Eastern Kosovo," 5
Economist, The (publication), 39
education, 47, 59, 72–74, 102
    Kosovo needed reform in, 149
    Kosovo parallel system of, 73–74
    Kosovo Serb primary school
        enrollments, 102
    Kosovo Serbs and, 44, 73
    Ottoman Turks and, 44
    See also universities
Egypt, 10
Egyptians (Roma in Kosovo), 104
Eide, Kai, 108, 111, 113
ELIAMEP (Greek think tank), 126
emigration, xv, 6, 7, 45–46, 52
    of Kosovo Serbs, 35–36, 56, 58–60,
        61–62, 92, 98, 100–101, 102, 103–4
    See also diasporas, Albanian; refugees
Enverism, 76–77
epic poems, 10, 21–23, 45

ESDP (European Security and Defense Policy), 114, 134, 138
ESI (European Stability Initiative), 101–2
ethnic Albania. *See* Greater Albania
ethnic cleansing, xvii, 3, 70, 71, 82, 93, 104, 124
ethnic minorities, 15, 41, 44, 54, 135
   expulsion of, from postwar Yugoslavia, 52
   in Kosovo, post–1999, 3, 104–5, 109
   in Kosovo 2008, 112 (map)
   Macedonia and, 4
   See also specific groups
EU. *See* European Union
EULEX, 114, 134–35, 139, 142, 145, 146, 147, 148
euro, xv, 98, 101, 105
Euro-Atlantic integration, xv
European Community, 130–31. *See also* European Union
European Council on Foreign Relations, 139
European Security and Defense Policy, 114, 134, 138
European Stability Initiative, 101–2
European Union, 79
   foreign policy of, 134–35
   Kosovo and, xiii, xv, 94, 97, 114–15, 116, 124, 128, 130, 134–35, 136, 138, 139
   Kosovo's independence declaration and, 140, 142, 145, 147, 148, 150
   Serbia and, 150
   Special Representative to Bosnia, 124
   Western Balkans and, xiii, xv, xvii, 128–30
EUSR (European Union's Special Representative), 114, 124, 147

families and blood feuds, 28, 29
Fascism, 7, 12, 77
Feith, Pieter, 114, 115, 147
Felgenhauer, Pavel, 131–32
Ferizaj/Uroševac, 30
"Field of Blackbirds." *See* Kosovo: battle for; Gazimestan
financial pyramid ("Ponzi") schemes, 80
First World War. *See* World War I
Fischer, Bernd, 47, 48
Flag Day (Albanian national day), 38, 81
flags, 27, 31, 98, 119, 144, 145
Flanders, 134
foreign investment, 148
France, 40, 41, 96, 100, 135
Franz Ferdinand, archduke, 40
Frashëri, Mithat, 10
freedom of movement, 109
Fushë Kosova/Kosovo Polje, 64–65. *See also* Kosovo: battle for

Galica, Shota, 43
Garašanin, Ilija, 36–37
gastarbeiters (guest workers), 16, 105, 106–7
Gaza, 127
Gazimestan, 67
Gelbard, Robert, 81, 82
"genocide," 62–63. *See also* ethnic cleansing
geography, xiii, 127, 138
geopolitics, 127, 138
Georgia (republic), 128, 132–33
Germans, ethnic minority in Yugoslavia, 15, 41, 44, 52
Germany, 46, 77
   ethnic Serbs in, 16
   Kosovo Albanian diaspora in, 3, 117, 122
   Kosovo's independence and, 135, 139
   Serbian diaspora in, 16
   World War I and, 40
   World War II and, 47, 52
   See also Nazis
Gërvalla, Jusuf and Bardhosh, 77
Gheg dialect, 9, 120
Gjakova. *See* Djakovica/Gjakova
Gnjilane/Gjilan, 102, 109
Gojbulja, 143
Goranis, 3, 104–5
   Kosovo areas (2008) of, 112 (map)
Gora region, 104
Goraždevac/Gorazhdevc, 92, 102
Gostivar, 4
Gračanica/Graçanica, 92
   as Kosovo Serb enclave, 102, 109
   church of, 19
Grdelica Bridge, 89
Great Britain. *See* Britain
Great Depression (1930s), 45
Greater Albania, 4, 7, 12, 43, 47, 48, 76, 117, 118, 119–22
   Albanian nationalists' view of, 120
Greater Croatia, 119
Greater Kosovo, 4, 121
Greater Serbia, 119
Great Migration (1690), 33–34
Great Powers, 38–39
Greece, 38, 117
   Albanian nationalism and, 10
   Albanians in, 6, 7, 120
   Balkan war of 1912 and 1913 and, 37, 38
   independence war of, 35
   Kosovo independence and, 139
   national identity and, 9
   Turkish population exchange with (1923), 46
Greek Orthodox Church, 9, 118
guest workers, 16, 105, 106–7
Gunjia, Maxim, 133
Gypsies. *See* Roma

Habsburg dynasty, 33, 34
Hague war crimes tribunal (ICTY), 78,
    90, 92, 142
Haliti, Xhavit, 85
Haradinaj, Ramush, 77–78, 80, 84
health care, 55–56, 74, 102
Helsinki Final Act, 86
Hercegovina, xvii, 19, 41. *See also* Bosnia
Hill, Chris, 84
history, 18–29
Holbrooke, Richard, 82, 83, 84
Hotel Grand (Pristina), 79
Hoxha, Enver, 8, 25, 48, 49, 76, 118
Hoxhaj, Enver, 149
humanitarian organizations, 74, 87
human rights abuses, 71. *See also*
    ethnic cleansing
Human Rights Watch, 89
Hungarians, ethnic, 15, 41, 44, 52, 54, 135
Hungary, 14, 32
Hysa, Ylber, 151

Ibar/Ibër River, 110
    as Kosovo Albanian–Serb boundary
        line, 101, 102
ICO. *See* International Civilian Office
ICR. *See* International Civilian
    Representative
identification papers, xv, 99–100, 101, 109
IKS (Kosovo Stability Initiative), 106
illegal migrants, xv
illiteracy, 55
Illyrians, 18
IMF (International Monetary Fund), 105
India, 150
Indonesia, xviii, 114
Institute for Advanced Studies
    (Kosovo), 148
Institute for Albanian Studies, 151
Institute of Statistics (Albania), 6
International Civilian Office (ICO), 114,
    139, 142, 145, 146, 147, 148
International Civilian Representative
    (ICR), 114, 115
    power of, 115–16
International Criminal Tribunal for the
    Former Yugoslavia (ICTY). *See*
    Hague war crimes tribunal
international community
    Balkan wars of 1990s and, 68, 83, 87
    Bosnia's recognition by, 124
    Kosovo's declaration of
        independence and, 145
    Kosovo's importance to, xiii–xix
    Kosovo's March 2004 riots and,
        110–11
    Kosovo's move to independence and,
        113–15
    Kosovo's rebuilding and, 97–98, 108

Kosovo's self-government standards
    and, 108–16
Kosovo's status and, 127–39
Kosovo war intervention and, 68,
    71, 87
    See also diplomacy; European
    Community; NATO; United
    Nations; *specific nations*
International Court of Justice (ICJ), 127
Internet, 117, 122, 149
Ioannina, 7, 117
Iraq war, xv, 135
Israel, 127
Istanbul, 10, 25
Italians, expulsion of, from Istria, 52
Italy, 28, 41, 139
    Albanians in, 6, 7
    invasion of Albania by, 46–47, 48
    Yugoslavia and, 12, 52

Jajce, 48
Jakšić, Marko, 145
Janina. *See* Ioannina
Jashari, Adem, 27, 78, 80, 81
Jashari, Kaqusha, 66
Jasharis, 28
Java (newspaper), 120
Jews, 17, 46
journalism, 98, 110, 122
Junik, 43

kaçaks (bandits), 42, 43, 45, 78
Kac̆anik/Kaçanik gorge, battle at
    (1690), 33
Kačanik/Kaçanik parliament votes at
    (1990), 69
Kadare, Ismail, 24–25, 27, 118, 120
Kalashnikov rifles, 80
Kanun (Canon), 28, 29
Karadžić, Vuk, 21, 41
Karaganov, Sergei, 137
Kastriot, Gjergj. *See* Skanderberg
KDOM (Kosovo Diplomatic Observer
    Mission), 83
Kelmendi, Migjen, 56–57, 119–20
KFOR (NATO-led Kosovo force), 91, 95,
    96, 101, 103, 147, 148
    March 2004 violence and, 110
Kičevo, 121
KK (Kosovo Committee), 42, 43
KLA. *See* Kosovo Liberation Army
Knaus, Gerald, 101–2
Koha Ditore (daily), 85, 143
Koriša/Korisha, civilian bombing deaths,
    89
Kosovo
    aerial bombardment of, 87, 88, 89
    Ahtisaari plan and, 108, 111, 113–16,
        136–37, 139, 145

Kosovo (*continued*)
  Albanian cultural/economic relations
      with, 122–23
  Albanian espionage trial (1956) and, 51
  Albanian presidential/parliamentary
      elections (1992) and, 70, 72
  Albanian-Serbian conflict in, 51–52
  Albanian shadow government in, 72–73
  Albanian union opposition in, 119
  Albanianization of, 53–54, 57, 59, 99
  anti-Albanian furor in, 66
  as autonomous region, 49, 53
  battle for (1912), 38
  battle of (1389), 20, 23, 24–25, 33, 39
  blood feuds and 28, 29
  borders (modern) of, 4, 5, 30, 43,
      52–53, 123, 125–26, 130
  border sealing (1948) of, 51
  Bosniak Muslims in, 17
  colonization by Serbs in, 44–45, 47,
      51–52
  communist rule in, 51, 58, 69, 75
  cultural development of, 56
  demographic changes in, 33–34,
      44–46, 55–56, 59
  diplomatic recognition of, xvii, 135,
      139, 148, 150
  economy of, 94, 105–7, 109, 122–23,
      148–50
  education and, 44, 72–74, 102, 149
  elections and, 95, 141–42
  ethnic minorities (2008) in, 112 (map)
  ethnic population statistics for, 1–2, 3,
      4, 15, 38, 104–5
  European interests in, 128–37. *See also*
      European Union
  flag of, 31, 98, 119, 144
  founding myth of, 27–28
  geography and, 127, 128
  golden age (1970s) of, 55–60
  government-in-exile of, 73
  government standards for, 108–16
  Greater Albania and, 120
  Great Migration from, 33–34
  history and, 18–29, 30, 32–33, 37, 38, 39
  house reconstruction aid in, 45
  independence declaration (1991) of,
      69, 77
  independence declaration (2008) of,
      xiii, xvii, xviii, 94–95, 96, 115, 135,
      140–51
  independence goal of, 111, 113–14,
      123–24, 126, 127–28, 130–39
  independence movements in, 76, 131
  international community and,
      97–98, 108
  interwar issues in, 44–46
  key events and dates affecting, 32–33,
      69, 79–80, 95–96

  land reform in, 45
  local elections in, 93–94
  Macedonian border fluidity with, 4
  map of, xiv
  Milošević policies and, 61, 64–67
  mineral resources of, 149
  Montenegrins in, 15, 38, 51
  name of, 30–32
  national identity and, 99–100, 119–20
  new challenges faced by, 150–51
  Ottoman Empire and, 14, 19, 23, 32,
      34, 117
  Partisan control of, 49
  as phantom republic, 69–73
  police service of, 95
  post-1999 non-Albanians in, 104
  post-1999 rebuilding of, 93–107
  poverty line in, 106–7
  regional position of, 117–26
  regions of, 30–32
  self-government and, 108–16
  Serb and Montenegrin post–World
      War II dominance in, 51
  Serb churches and monasteries in,
      19, 23–24
  Serb control of, xix, 38, 39, 67–68,
      100, 101
  Serb emigration from, 35–36, 56,
      58–60, 61–62, 92, 98, 100–101, 102,
      103–4
  Serbian Academy genocide charges
      against, 62–63
  as Serbian Jerusalem, 24, 147
  Serbian-Turkish war and, 35
  Serbia's interests in, 10, 11, 12–13, 14,
      16, 18–19, 37, 65
  Serb loss of status in, 59
  significance of, xiii–xvix
  600th anniversary celebration of 1389
      battle of, 67–68
  small factories in, 149
  social problems in, 98
  square mileage of, 127
  Standards before Status for, 108–9, 110
  student protests in, 53, 57–58, 60–61, 76
  UN interim administration in, 94–96,
      99, 100, 101, 105–7, 113, 116
  unrest (1878–1912) in, 37
  unskilled labor market in, 148–49
  violence of March 2004 in, 102, 108,
      109–11
  world politics and, 127–39
  World War I and, 40–41, 44, 103
  World War II division of, 47, 48, 49,
      51–52
  youthful population of, 16
  Yugoslavia's dissolution and, 65–66
  Yugoslav status of, xv, xvii, xviii, 41,
      42–54, 57, 58, 65, 130

See also Kosovo Albanians; Kosovo
     Serbs; Kosovo war
Kosovo Albanians, 1–11, 14–15, 18, 20, 24
     Ahtisaari plan and, 115
     armed resistance after 1918, 42–43
     as Catholics, 7, 33
     citizenship status of, 3
     deaths from aerial bombing of, 89–90
     deportations of, 88
     diasporas of, 3, 6, 7, 11, 45–46, 73, 74,
          77, 81, 88–89
     economic problems of, 105–7
     education and, 55, 59
     ethnic cleansing actions by, 91–93, 98,
          100, 104
     forced deportation (ethnic cleansing)
          of, 88–89, 90
     Greater Albania and, 117, 118
     history and, 24–29, 30–41, 42, 47
     identity and, 26–27, 41, 44
     Kosovo borders and, 123
     Kosovo control by, 57
     Kosovo identity and, 9, 17, 119–20
     Kosovo independence and, 124, 140,
          142, 151
     Kosovo independence declaration
          and, 144, 145
     Kosovo's golden age (1970s) and,
          55–60
     Kosovo war and, 81, 85–86, 88–89
     Macedonian Albanians and, 4
     March 2004 violence and, 109–11
     marginalization of, 51
     middle class and, 118
     as Muslims, 8, 15, 24, 25, 33, 34
     nationalist culture of, 73–74, 76, 119
     Paraćin murders and, 66
     parallel institutions of, 71
     in police service, 95
     population growth of, 55–56, 59, 105
     population percentage of, 2, 3,
          48–49, 59
     post–1999 disparities in numbers
          of, 102
     post–1999 status of, 93–94, 99
     post–1999 violence and, 91–92, 98
     post–independence outlook for, 149–50
     post–World War II status of, 51, 52, 130
     protests by, 53–54, 60–61, 67–68, 76
     as refugees in Albania, 88
     religions of, 7–8
     resistance to Serbians by, 42, 67
     self-determination and, xviii–xix
     Serbian dislocation of, 35
     Serbian massacres of, 39–40, 41, 42
     settlement regions of, 3–4, 5
     settlement regions of (2008), 112 (map)
     shadow government of, 72–73
     standards for government and, 109

     tax-raising system of, 73
     as World War II Partisans, 49
Kosovo and Metohija (Kosmet), 31
Kosovo Committee (KK), 42, 43
Kosovo Diplomatic Observer Mission
     (KDOM), 83
Kosovo Liberation Army (KLA/UCK),
     27, 75–79, 80
     disarmament of, 95–96
     first casualties of, 79
     first death in uniform of, 80–81
     forerunners of, 76
     growing strength of, 81–82
     Holbrooke-Milošević agreement
          and, 84
     key founders of, 58, 75–76, 77, 85,
          121, 141
     March 2004 violence and, 109–10
     military successes of, 75
     post–Kosovo war position of, 93,
          95–96
     Rambouillet talks and, 85–86
     reduced power of, 88
     terrorism and, 81, 82, 84
Kosovo Montenegrins, 2, 15, 38, 45, 51,
     59, 101
Kosovo Police Service (KPS), 95, 146
Kosovo Polje/Fushë Kosova, 64–65.
     See also Kosovo, battle of
Kosovo Protection Corps (KPC), 95–96, 109
Kosovo Serbs, 14, 15, 39, 62
     alleged atrocities against, 62–63, 92
     areas in post–1999 Kosovo of, 101,
          102–3, 123
     areas in 2008 of, 112 (map)
     colonization by, 44–45, 47, 51 52
     complaints of, 64–65
     diminished power of, 98
     dominance of, 39, 51, 61, 67–68, 98,
          100, 101
     education and, 44, 73, 104
     emigration of, 35–36, 56, 58–60, 61–62,
          92, 98, 100–101, 102, 103–4
     enclave of, 102, 109
     Kosovo Albanians' parallel lives
          with, 74
     Kosovo independence and, 133
     Kosovo independence declaration
          and, 143, 144, 145–46, 147, 148
     Kosovo war flight of, 82, 91, 92, 93
     Kosovo war reprisals against, 91–92
     loss of status of, 59
     March 2004 violence and, 109–11
     in police service, 95
     population percentage of, 2, 3, 32, 39,
          51, 56, 59, 60, 101–2, 104
     post–1999 disparities in numbers
          of, 102
     power shift to, 61

Kosovo Serbs (*continued*)
  reasons for staying in Kosovo of, 103
  violence against, 102–3
  as World War II refugees, 47, 51–52
Kosovo Stability Initiative (IKS), 106
Kosovo Statistical Office, 2, 3
Kosovo Verification Mission (KVM), 83,
  84, 87
Kosovo war, xiii, xvii, 27, 61, 75–92
  Albanian weapons/outbreak of, 80–81
  chaotic period following, 91–94
  civilian deaths in, 89–90
  death toll of, 87, 91
  Democratic League of Kosovo and, 69
  displaced persons from, 3, 100
  ethnic cleansing and, 82
  first death in uniform of, 80–81
  international diplomacy and, 82,
    83–84
  international opinion and, 89
  Kosovo Albanian expulsions and, 3,
    88–89
  massacres and, 88, 89–90
  NATO aerial bombardment, 75,
    87–88, 89, 90, 108, 137
  postwar events and, 93–107
  prologue to, 75–80
  Rambouillet talks and, 84–87
  reprisals following, 91–92
  Serbian counter-offensive, 82–83
  settlement terms for, 91
  terrorist acts and, 84, 88, 91
  UN war crimes tribunal, 78, 90
  Western intervention factors in, 68,
    71, 87
Kostić, Bratislav, 143
Kostovicova, Denisa, 44
Koštunica, Vojislav, 124, 141, 142, 145, 150
Kouchner, Bernard, 96
KPC. *See* Kosovo Protection Corps
KPS. *See* Kosovo Police Service
Kragujevac, 59
Krajina, Republic of Serbian, 13, 69
Kraljevo, 59
Krasniqi, Adrian, 80–82
Krasniqi, Jakup, 146
Krastev, Ivan, 98
Krstić, Branislav, 60–61
Kuçi, Ahmet, 149
Kumanovo, battle of (1912), 38
Kurdistan, xviii
Kurti, Albin, 80
KVM (Kosovo Verification Mission), 83,
  84, 87

Lajcak, Miroslav, 124
language
  Albanian, 9, 15, 17, 53, 101, 104
  Albanian standard literary, 118

Cyrillic alphabet and, 98, 100
  as defining national identity, 9, 17
  Gheg, Kosovar Albanian dialect, 120
  Kosovo divisions in, 101
  Serbian, 55, 73, 101, 104
  Tosk dialect, 9, 118
Lani, Remzi, 120–21
Lausanne Treaty (1923), 7, 46
Lavrov, Sergei, 136, 137
Lazar (Serbian hero), 20, 21–23, 25, 27,
  33, 39
LDK. *See* Democratic League of Kosovo
lead mines, 47
League of Prizren (1878), 36, 69
Lešak/Leshak, 5
Leskovac, 35, 89
Lëvizja Popullore e Kosovës (LPK). *See*
  Popular Movement for Kosova
Lex Duodecim Tabularum, 29
lignite, 149
Likošane/Likoshan, 81
London conference (1912), 38
LPK. *See* Popular Movement for Kosova
Lubonja, Fatos, 10, 25, 26

Macedonia, 32, 90, 117, 118, 121, 123
  Albanian Muslims in, 8, 33
  Albanian resistance in, 42
  Albanian settlement regions in, 3–4,
    121–22, 123
  Balkan war of 1912 effects on, 38
  conflict, 2001
  European Union and, 130
  Greater Albania and, 120
  Kosovo Albanian deportations to, 88
  Kosovo Albanian refugees in, 88
  Kosovo border with, 4, 52, 125
  migrations from, 45
  percentage of Albanians in, 4
  percentage of Serbs in, 14
  Serbian designs on, 10, 37, 89
  square mileage of, 127
  World War II and, 47
  as Yugoslav republic, xv, 41, 53
Macedonians, 4, 17
Makarije, Patriarch, 32
Malcolm, Noel, 34
Mandela, Nelson, 76
March 2004 violence (Kosovo), 102, 108,
  109–11
  casualties of, 110
Marković, Mira, 64
Marku, Adelina, 121
martyrs, 28, 78, 81
Marxist-Leninist groups, 58, 75, 76, 77
massacres, 39, 42, 88, 90
  Meja, 89–90
  Racak/Reçak, 90
  Srebrenica, 68, 87

Médecins Sans Frontières, 96
Medvedja/Medvegja (Serbia), 5
Meetings of Truth (Serbia), 66
Meja massacre, 89–90
Memorandum (of the Serbian Academy)
   1986, 62–63
Metohija/Rrafsh i Dukagjinit, 30, 48, 62, 147
Middle Ages, 18–20, 21, 25
Mijatović, Čedomil, 23
Milica (Lazar's widow), 21
Milošević, Slobodan, 16, 24, 44, 58, 64–70,
   131
   background of, 64
   consolidation of power by, 65–68
   Croatian and Bosnian wars and, 70, 71
   death of, 90
   fall of, 90, 141
   Kosovo power shift and, 61
   Kosovo war and, 81, 82–84, 85, 87,
      88–89, 91
   missteps of, 65
   power decline of, 70
   war crimes indictment of, 90
mining, 19, 47, 74, 82, 105
   Trepča workers' strike and, 67
minorities. *See* ethnic minorities;
      specific groups
Misha, Piro, 26, 27
Mitrovica, 30, 47, 110, 143, 145, 147
   concentration camp, 47
   post–Kosovo war division of,
      100–101, 102
   violence (2008) in, 123
Mlike, 105
Moldova, 132
Monastir/Bitola, 117
Montenegrins, 6, 17, 35, 51, 64
   massacre of Albanians by, 40
Montenegro, xv, 3, 12, 15, 19
   Albanian resistance in, 42
   Albanians in, 5–6, 7, 52–53
   Balkan war of 1912 and 1913 and,
      11, 37, 38
   bombing of, 75, 87, 90
   independence of (1878), 10, 35
   independence of (2006), 5, 12, 134
   Kosovo Albanian refugees in, 88
   Kosovo borders and, 52–53
   Kosovo cities under, 38
   Kosovo interests of, 10
   Milošević and, 16, 24, 44, 58, 64–70
   nationalism and, 35
   Serbs in, 13–14
   territorial size of, 127
   World War I and, 40
   as Yugoslav republic, xvii, 41, 53, 79, 99
Morocco, 127
Murad, sultan, 20, 21, 45
murders, after 1999, 98

Muslims, 14, 15
   Albanian, 7, 8, 9, 15, 25, 26, 27, 28, 32,
      33, 34, 36, 118
   Albanian émigrés to Turkey, 52
   Greek-Turkish population exchange
      and, 46
   Kosovo independence and, 150
   Kosovo religious schools and, 44
   migrations from Kosovo by, 45
   Montenegrin, 35
   national identity as, 17
   Ottoman conquest and, 32
   See also Bosniaks
Mussolini, Benito, 7, 12, 46

Nagorno-Karabakh, 132
national identity, 16–17
   Albanian, 29, 44, 118
   Kosovo Albanians and, 119
   religion defining, 9, 14, 17, 19, 21, 24,
      31, 32
   Serbian, 9, 21, 26
nationalist movements
   Albania and, 9–11, 26–27, 35, 36, 44,
      77, 119, 120–21
   breakaway regions and, 130–34, 135
   Montenegro and, 35
   Ottoman Empire and, 14, 35
   Slavs and, 37
   Slovenia and, 61, 67
   Yugoslavia and, 65–66, 67
   See also self-determination
NATO, xiii, 3, 83, 84, 85, 86, 90, 111, 135
   bombing of Yugoslavia by, 75, 87–88,
      89, 90, 108, 137
   Bulgaria and Romania as members
      of, xv, 128
   Kosovo as "NATO" state, 142
   peacekeeping troops and, 91, 95, 97,
      101, 103, 113, 134
   refugee camps and, 89
   Slovenia as member of, xv
   See also KFOR
Nazis, 7, 12, 46, 47, 48
Nemanja, Rastko. *See* Sava, St.
Nemanja, Stefan, 19
Nemanjić dynasty, 19–20, 21, 25, 32
Nikolić, Tomislav, 142
Niš, 15, 35, 59
   civilian bombing deaths in, 89
Nishliu, Rona, 74
North Mitrovica, 143, 145, 147
North Ossetia, 130, 133
Novi Pazar, 117
Novo Brdo/Novobërda, 19, 20
Nushi, Pajazit, 29

Obilić (settler village), 45
Obilić, Miloš, 20, 39, 45

Ohrid, 32
    Lake Ohrid, 3
"Old Albania," 47
"Old Serbia" (Kosovo and the Sandžak), 37
Olivera (Lazar's daughter), 20
Orahovac/Rahovec, 82
Organization for Security and
        Cooperation in Europe (OSCE),
        83, 91
    Kosovo institution building and, 94
organized crime, xv, 98, 114, 135
Orthodox Christians
    Albanian, 6, 7, 8
    Greeks, 9, 118
    Kosovar attacks against churches, 91
    Ottoman Empire and, 118
    Russian, 39
    See also Serbian Orthodox Church
OSCE. See Organization for Security and
        Cooperation in Europe
Ottoman Empire, 12, 28
    Albanians and, 7, 19, 25, 36, 37, 44,
        117, 120
    Albanians' power in, 9–10, 34–35
    decline of, 34–35
    end in Balkans of, 37
    Kosovo and, 14, 19, 23, 32, 34, 117
    nationalist movements and, 35, 44
    Serbs and, 12, 18, 20, 21, 24–25, 32,
        35, 37, 42
    siege of Vienna (1683) by, 33
    Tanzimat reforms of, 35
    Young Turk revolution in, 37, 39
    See also Turkey

Pajaziti, Zahir, 79
Panda Café (Peć/Peja), 84
Paraćin murders (1987), 65–66
Partisans, 13, 48, 49, 51, 61, 71–72
passport-free zone, xv
Peć/Peja, 30, 38, 84
    anti-Serb violence in, 102–3
    Kosovo Albanian expulsions from, 88
Peć/Peja, Patriarchate of, 19, 30, 32
    abolishment of (1766), 34
Petritsch, Wolfgang, 84
Piccolomini, Eneo, 33
PISG (Provisional Institutions of
        Self-Government), 108
Pliev, Alan, 133
Podgorica, 6
Poles, ethnic, 52
Polluzha, Shaban, 49
"Ponzi" schemes, 80
Popović, Justin, 24
Popular Movement for Kosova (LPK), 76,
        78, 79, 80
population exchanges, 7, 46
population growth, 55–56, 59, 105

population shifts, 34
Požarevac, 64
Prekaz, 27, 28, 78, 81
Preševo/Presheva, 5, 43, 52, 123
Preševo Valley, 5, 123
Princip, Gavrilo, 40
Prishtina, Hasan, 42, 43
Pristina, 25, 30, 31, 45, 72, 77, 102
    Albanian deportations from, 88
    concentration camp in, 47
    independence declaration celebration
        in, 141, 143–44, 145
    intimidation of Serb residents of, 98
    as Kosovo capital city, 101
    March 2004 riots and, 109–11
    modernization of, 56
Pristina University, 15
    as Albanian institution, 53
    student protests at, 53, 57–58, 80
Prizren, 30, 34, 36
    Albanian espionage trial in, 51
    Bosnian Muslims in, 104
    burning of Kosovo Serbian houses
        in, 91–92
    Gora region south of, 104
    and Turkish in, 56–57
Prokuplje, 35
property rights, 109
protests. See student protests
Provisional Institutions of
        Self-Government (PISG), 108
Putin, Vladimir, 132, 137, 138

Qemal, Ismail, 37
Qosja, Rexhep, 37, 72
Quebec, xviii, 134

Račak/Reçak massacre, 90
Račak/Reçak offensive, 84
Radio Free Europe, 138
Rrafsh i Dukagjinit/Metohija, 30
Rambouillet talks (1999), 84–87, 94, 115
    key proposal of, 85–86
Ranković, Aleksandar, 51, 53
Raška, 19. See also Sandžak
reconciliation rituals (Albania, 1990s),
        28–29
refugees, 14, 15, 16, 35, 91, 110, 132
    Kosovo war, xvii, 3, 82, 87, 88, 89–90,
        91, 94, 100
    UN agency for, 82, 87, 88, 94, 101
    World War II, 47, 51–52
religion
    Albanians and, 6, 7–9, 25–26, 31, 32,
        33, 34, 118, 150
    as defining identity, 9, 17, 32
    Serbs and, 9, 14, 17, 19, 21, 24, 31
    See also Catholics; Muslims; Orthodox
        Christians

Republika Srpska (RS), 69–70, 124
Resolution 1244 (UN Security Council),
    91, 94, 95, 137, 142, 145, 147
Rexhepi, Bajram, 110
Roma, 14, 91, 110
    in Kosovo, 2, 3, 104
    Kosovo war displacement of, 100
Roman Catholics. *See* Catholics
Romania, xv, 128, 135
Roman law, 29
RS. *See* Republika Srpska
Rugova, Ibrahim, 31, 78, 79, 81, 85
    background of, 71–72
    Holbrooke's diplomatic mission
        and, 82
    nonviolence strategy of, 70–71
    post–Kosovo war popularity of, 96
rule of law, 109, 114, 128, 145
    collapse in Kosovo of, 93
    democracy and, 97
Russia, 37, 46
    Albanian state and, 39
    Kosovo independence and, 113, 114,
        131–33, 136–37, 138–39, 140–41,
        145, 150
    Kosovo war and, xviii, 84, 85, 87, 90,
        91, 135–36, 137
    threat of breakaway republics to,
        xviii, 130–31
Russo-Turkish War, 126
Rwanda, 127

SAA (Stabilization and Association
    Agreement), 128, 130
St. Sava's church, 147
Salonika front, 41
Samardžić, Slobodan, 146
Sandžak, 15, 19, 117–18
Sarajevo, 125
    Franz Ferdinand's assassination in,
        40, 46
    siege of (1992–95), 68, 70
Sarkozy, Nicolas, 96
Sava, St., 19, 21
Scandinavia, 3, 16
schools. *See* education
"Schengen" Europe, xv
Schwandner-Sievers, Stephanie, 27, 29
Seapi, Hamdije, 105
Second World War. *See* World War II
Security Council. *See* United Nations
Sejdiu, Fatmir, 146
self-determination, 127
    Badinter Commission and, 131
    Kosovo and, 94, 124, 126, 131
    precedent and, xviii–xix, 131–32, 134
Self-Determination movement. *See*
    Vetëvendosje
separatist regions, xviii, 130–34, 135

    Kosovo as precedent for, 130
    See also self-determination
Serbia, 12–17
    Albanian occupation by, 38
    Albanian settlement region of, 5, 120
    Balkan war of 1912 and 1913 and, 11,
        37, 38, 39
    bombings of, 68, 75, 87, 89, 90, 108, 137
    border demilitarized zone, 43
    Bosnia and, 32–33, 69–70, 124, 125
    Chetniks and, 49, 51
    communism and, 20, 64–65, 66
    epic poems of, 21–23
    expansion of, 35, 69–70
    government's collapse (2008) in, 150
    Greater Serbia and, 119
    historical status of, 12–13, 14, 17, 18, 40
    independence (1878) of, 10, 14, 23, 35
    international sanctions against, 79
    Kosovo's annexation by (1945), 49
    Kosovo's historical relations with,
        xviii–xix, 11, 12–13, 18–19, 30–41,
        123–24, 130
    Kosovo's independence and, 138, 140,
        141, 146–48, 151
    Kosovo's modern borders and, 52
    Kosovo's name and, 31
    Kosovo's parliamentary
        representation in, 57, 65
    Kosovo's 1974 status in, 57
    Kosovo's post–1999 status and, 99,
        100, 111, 113
    Kosovo's reconquest by (1918), 42–43
    Kosovo war and, 3, 61, 75–92, 81–92,
        135–36
    Milošević and, 16, 24, 44, 58, 61, 64–70
    national identity and, 9, 21, 26
    Ottoman Empire's collapse and, 37
    population (2002) of, 13
    population decline of, 16
    presidential election (2008) in, 142
    rebellion (1804) of, 18, 35, 62
    rebellion (1941) of, 62
    Sandžak region of, 15, 19, 117–18
    UN administration of Kosovo and, 94
    UN Resolution 1244 and, 137
    World War I and, 40–41
    World War II and, 47
    Yugoslavia's dissolution and, 79,
        84, 131
    as Yugoslav republic, xv, 12–13, 15,
        51, 63, 79
    See also Balkan wars (1990s); Kosovo
        Serbs; Serbs
Serbian Academy of Sciences and Arts, 62
Serbian Communist Party, 64–65
Serbian language, 55, 73, 101, 104
Serbian Orthodox Church, 14, 17, 21,
    23–24, 30–34, 39, 67, 91, 118

Serbian Orthodox Church (*continued*)
  exodus of Kosovo Serbs and, 61–62
  founder of, 19
  Kosovo Albanians' violence against
    churches, 110
  Kosovo independence and, 147
  national identity and, 9
  protection of Kosovo churches and
    monasteries of, 113
  shift in center of, 34
Serbian Radical Party, 142
Serbian revolt (1804), 18, 35, 62
Serbian-Turkish wars (1876–1878), 35
Serbs, 1, 5, 12–17, 38, 120
  in Bosnia, 13, 62, 91, 125
  in Croatia, 13, 14, 33, 62, 63
  Greater Serbia and, 199
  living abroad, 3, 14, 15–16, 62
  in Macedonia, 14
  migrations of, 13, 14, 15, 18, 33, 35
  Miloševic's popularity among, 65
  in Montenegro, 13–14
  move back to Serbia of (1878), 35–36
  religion as defining identity of, 9, 14,
    17, 19, 21, 24, 31
  Yugoslavia's dissolution and, 131
  as Yugoslavia's predominant
    group, 51
  See also Kosovo Serbs; Serbia
Serbs, Croats, and Slovenes, Kingdom of,
  12, 41. *See also* Yugoslavia
Šešelj, Vojislav, 142
Shkodër/Skadar, 6, 7, 10, 42, 117
  Montenegrin control of, 38
  shkolla shqipe (Albanian schools), 44
Sicily, 28
Skadar. *See* Shkodër/Skadar
Skanderberg (Albanian hero), 25–26, 27,
  29, 31
  SS batallion Skanderbeg, 48
Skopje, 4, 5, 8, 19, 33, 109, 118
Slavs, 18, 19, 31, 33, 35, 104
  Albanians differentiated from, 118
  nationalism of, 37
Slovakia, 135
Slovenes, 17
Slovenia, 41, 61, 67, 99
  EU/NATO membership of, xv
  independence declaration (1991) of, 68
  industry and, 55
  Serbian charges against, 66
  as Yugoslav republic, 53, 105
Slovenian war, 61, 68
Smerderevo, fall of (1459), 32
smuggling, 98
Sokolević clan, 32
Sokollu, Mehmed, 32
South Ossetia, 132, 133
Soviet Union

collapse of, xvii, xviii, 130, 132, 137
  Yugoslav split with, 49
  See also Russia
Spain, xviii, 135
Special Representative of the Secretary
  General. *See* SRSG
Srebrenica massacre, 68, 87
Sremski Karlovci, as Serbian Orthodox
  center, 34
Srpska, Republic of. *See* Republika Srpska
SRSG (Special Representative of the
  Secretary General), 94, 95, 96,
  97, 145
SS battalion, Skanderbeg, 48
Stabilization and Association Agreement,
  128, 130
Stalin, Joseph, 25
Stambolić, Ivan, 64–65, 66
Standards before Status (Kosovo
  post-2003 policy), 108–9, 111
  goals of, 109
Staro Gracko/Gracko e Vjetër, 91
Stefan (Lazar's son), 20
Štimlje/Shtime, 84
Štrpce/Shtërpca, 92, 102
Struga, 3
student protests (1968), 53
student protests (1981), 57–58, 60–61, 76
  significance of, 58
student protests (1997), 80
Stuttgart, 77
Sufis, 8
Suleiman the Magnificent, 32
Sunni Muslims, 8
Surroi, Veton, 85, 86, 92, 123, 125
  assessment of UNMIK by, 96, 97
Switzerland, 17, 92, 106–7
  ethnic Albanians in, 3, 77, 117, 122
  ethnic Serbs in, 16

Tadić, Boris, 141, 142, 150
Taiwan, 134, 151
Tanzimat reforms, 35
Tatarstan, 130
telephone dialing codes, 99
television, 122, 125
Teresa, Mother, 8, 74
  street, 145
terrorism, xv, xvii
Tetovo, 4
Thaçi, Hashim, 77, 85, 86
  as Kosovo's prime minister, 141–42,
    143, 144, 146
Thessalonika, 5, 20, 38, 41, 128
Tibet, xviii, 134
Tirana, 25, 43, 138
Tito, Josip Broz, 13, 48, 49, 65
  death of, 57, 61
Toplica, 35

Tosk dialect, 9, 118
tourism, 55, 123
Transnistria, 132
Trepča/Trepça mines, 47, 74, 82
    Kosovo's economy and, 105
    workers' strike in, 67
Tskhinvali, 133
Tudjman, Franjo, 70
Turkey
    ethnic Albanians in, 7, 52
    Greek population exchange with, 46
    migrants from Yugoslavia to, 46, 52
    See also Ottoman Empire
Turkish language, 56
Turks, 10, 44, 104
Tuzi/Tuz, 6, 53

UCK. See Kosovo Liberation Army
Ukrainians, ethnic, 52
Ulcinj/Ulqin, 6, 53
UNHCR, 82, 87, 88, 94, 101
United Nations, 2, 127, 135
    Ahtisaari plan blockage in, 113–14,
        115, 136–37
    bombing of Serbia and, 87
    Kosovo and, 80, 110–11
    Kosovo independence and, xvii, xviii,
        138, 139, 141
    Kosovo peacekeeping and, 91, 92,
        93–94
    Kosovo war settlement terms and, 91
    refugee agency, 82, 87, 88, 94, 101
    Security Council Resolution 1244, 91,
        94, 95, 137, 142, 145, 147
    Srebrenica massacre and, 68
    Yugoslav war crimes tribunal, 78, 90,
        92, 142
United Nations Interim Administration
    Mission in Kosovo (UNMIK),
        92, 94–96, 99, 100, 101, 125, 146,
        147, 148
    assessment of, 96–97
    economic failure of, 105–7
    end of mission of, 113, 116
    four pillars of, 94
    key accomplishments of, 95
    Kosovo "Standards before Status"
        policy of, 108–9, 111
    March 2004 violence and, 110, 111
    two phases of, 108
United States
    Bush (G.H.W.) warning to Milošević
        and, 71
    Albanians in, 3, 6, 7
    ethnic Serbs in, 16
    Kosovo Albanians' trust in, 115, 144
    Kosovo charities in, 45
    Kosovo declaration of independence
        and, 144–45, 150

Kosovo policies of, 128, 135, 136, 138,
    142, 144
Kosovo war and, 82, 83, 84, 86, 90
Serbs attack embassy of, 147
Serbs in, 16
universities, 4, 15, 46
    Kosovo parallel institutions, 74
    Kosovo student protests and, 53,
        57–58, 76, 80
UNMIK. See United Nations Interim
    Administration Mission in Kosovo
Uroševac/Ferizaj, 30
Ušće rally (1989), 66
Ushtria Çlirimtare e Kosovës (UCK). See
    Kosovo Liberation Army

vaccinations, 55
Valjevo, 15
Vasa, Pashko, 9
Velimirović, Nikolaj, 24
Veremis, Thanos, 126
Vetëvendosje, 80
Victor Emmanuel, king of Italy and
    Albania, 46–47
Vienna, siege of (1683), 33
Vienna talks (2005), 111, 136
visa policy, 128
Visoki Dečani church, 19, 30
Vlassi, Azem, 66
Vlora, 38, 123
Vojvodina, 15, 32, 34, 41, 51, 53, 130
    ethnic Serbs in, 62
    expulsion of ethnic minorities from, 52
    Milošević and, 66
Vranje, 35
Vučitrn/Vushtrri, 47
Vukovar, siege of (1991), 68

Walker, William, 84
war crimes, 78, 90, 92, 110, 114, 142
Western Balkans, xiii–xix, 1, 128–30, 141
    definition of, xv, xvii
    geographical position of, xiii, xv
    map of, xvi
    map of Europe and, 129
    postwar success story of, xvii
White Russians, 43
World War I, 15, 39, 40–41, 44
World War II, 7, 13, 15, 43, 44
    Kosovo's status following, 30, 130
    Serb refugees from Kosovo and, 47,
        51–52
    Yugoslavia and, 46–49, 51, 52, 118
Writers' Union (Kosovo), 72

Xhakli, Kushtrim, 149

Yasmann, Victor, 138
Young Turks, 37, 39

Yugoslavia, 12–13, 15, 42–54, 55–70
  Albanians and, 54, 118
  classification of peoples in, 53–54
  communism and, 13, 49, 51, 61, 65
  component nations of, xv, xvii, 41,
    51, 53–54
  component remaining nations of, 79, 99
  disintegration of, xvii, 62–63, 65–70,
    130–31
  ethnic minorities and, 41, 44, 52
  Federal Republic of Yugoslavia as
    successor to, 79, 94
  formation of, 12–13, 15
  foundations for new, 48–49
  golden age (1970s) of, 55–60, 76
  Kosovo's place in, 42–54, 57, 58, 105,
    123, 130
  map (1945–1991) of, 50
  migrants from, 45–46
  minorities' expulsion from, 52
  nationalist growth in, 65–66, 67
  NATO bombing of, 75, 87–88, 89, 90,
    108, 137
  1974 constitution of, 57
  Partisans and, 13, 48, 49, 51, 71–72
  security services of, 51
  telephone dialing code of, 99
  unity move in, 45
  Western Balkans comprising former
    states of, xv, xvii
  World War II and, 46–49, 51, 52, 118
Yugoslavia, Federal Republic of, 79, 94.
    See also Montenegro; Serbia
Yugoslav war crimes tribunal, 78, 90,
    92, 142
Yugoslav wars. See Balkan wars (1990s)

Zagreb, 125, 138
Zeka, Kadri, 77
Žiča (Sandžak), 19
Zog, King of the Albanians, 43, 47, 48
Zogu, Ahmed. See Zog